TIME AND TIMING IN THE CLASSROOM

TIME AND TIMING IN THE CLASSROOM
The Cornerstone of Any Child's Education

Rowland Creitz

Copyright © 2007 by Rowland Creitz

All rights reserved. No part of this book shall be reproduced or transmitted in any form or by any means, electronic, mechanical, magnetic, photographic including photocopying, recording or by any information storage and retrieval system, without prior written permission of the publisher. No patent liability is assumed with respect to the use of the information contained herein. Although every precaution has been taken in the preparation of this book, the publisher and author assume no responsibility for errors or omissions. Neither is any liability assumed for damages resulting from the use of the information contained herein.

ISBN 0-7414-4132-2

Editor: Marial Shea
Book design: R-house Design
Cover photograph: Getty Images/American Images Inc.
Author photograph: Philbrick Photography

Published by:

INFINITY
PUBLISHING.COM

1094 New DeHaven Street, Suite 100
West Conshohocken, PA 19428-2713
Info@buybooksontheweb.com
www.buybooksontheweb.com
Toll-free (877) BUY BOOK
Local Phone (610) 941-9999
Fax (610) 941-9959

Printed in the United States of America

Printed on Recycled Paper

Published July 2007

Contents

Introduction — 7

PART I A CHRONIC CONDITION
1. Contradictions and Paradoxes — 11
2. The Good Ol' Days — 15
3. The Nature of Kids — 20
4. A Call to Arms — 24
5. The "Experts" Strike Back — 29
6. Sirens of the Deep — 35
7. Few Caesars to Be Found — 41
8. The Caregivers — 47
9. The Child's Structure — 53
10. Fooling with Mother Nature — 59
11. Mindless Momentum — 64
12. A World of Change — 71
13. The Decline of Rome — 77
14. The Simplicity of the Problem — 85

PART II THE COMMON THREAD OF TIME
15. First Impressions — 91
16. The Meat of the Subject — 95
17. The Big Mo — 101
18. *The* Skill, the *Only* Skill — 106
19. As Easy As ABC — 111
20. The Reading-Writing Connection — 115
21. Chicken Scratching — 121
22. I Before E — 126

23 Matter Over Mind	130
24 Science Is Doing	136
25 The Three Musketeers	140
26 Making Jack a Dull Boy	145
27 Speeka dee English?	150
28 Nerds and Technophobes	157
29 An Ounce of Prevention	163
30 Fertile Soil	168
31 All the Time in the World	172
Index	175
Author's Notes	180

Introduction

IT IS TEMPTING TO COMPARE past and present reform efforts in American education to a rat on a wheel. Regardless of the rat's effort, it goes nowhere. Another comparison, and perhaps better, would be to a snail or, better yet, a glacier. A glacier sometimes moves very slowly forward but sometimes it retreats. Maintaining the status quo in education or accepting gradual or erratic improvement is unacceptable in today's fast-changing world. Not only do our children need an improved and excellent education now, the present system wastes an incredible amount of taxpayers' money. Clearly, something dramatic and different must be done to create a *huge and lasting* improvement.

The purpose of this book is not to cover exhaustively every school issue. Rather, first it identifies the main obstacle to success. Although just *one*, the obstacle is like a common thread in that it has a devastating impact on every facet of education. Second, the book identifies the changes that must be made. Again few in number, the changes are scandalously easy to implement and they foster immediate, obvious and substantial success.

At times the book may seem to be only about younger school children. However, many mistakes are made in the early school years and they are big ones. These mistakes then follow the students right up the line and have a bigger impact, year by year. Thus, the obstacle and solutions discussed apply to students of all ages. This is not a pie-in-the-sky document. As will be revealed, the formula to ensure school success is known and used in a scattered fashion throughout the country. In essence, everything suggested in this book to improve education has been done successfully by various educators, including myself. The personal anecdotes that are included simply reflect experiences that are typical for any veteran teacher. They and the other information in the book point to the tragedy of underachieving and failing children. We know what to do, but we *don't* do it.

∼

PART I

A CHRONIC CONDITION

I was only a first year teacher yet Angie stuck out like a sore thumb. She was shy, smaller than the other twenty-seven third-grade students and they treated her like a kid sister. Angie wasn't close to third grade level in her academic achievement and needed daily help. I remember best her teeth. They were all her first set. Then, I didn't know how important a clue that was.

∽

Leroy perhaps was the brightest child in my first-grade class. He showed all the normal signs of beginning to read, such as mastering the alphabet and consonant sounds. The problem was his timing. He had just turned seven and it was the end of the school year. Leroy's parents were very loving, high-achieving professionals with advanced degrees (one a doctorate) and had enrolled their son in formal schools since age three. According to conventional wisdom, Leroy not only should have been reading already, he should have been at the top of his class.

1

Contradictions and Paradoxes
The Puzzling Status Quo

> *"The schools are letting us down at a time when the nation is in great peril... reform is urgently needed and must not be delayed."*
>
> — Admiral Hyman Rickover
> United States Navy
> (1900–1986)

PEOPLE ARE BORN TO LEARN. From birth, human minds act as limitless sponges to absorb the surrounding world. Economics, mathematics, the sciences, transportation, sociology and agriculture are just a few of the many subject areas humans learn about directly or indirectly each day. It used to be accepted that formal learning stopped at the schoolroom door, usually at a young age. Today it is recognized that formal or informal learning should be a lifetime activity. Students middle-aged and older are learning to read, completing high school programs and getting college degrees. As humans learn at any and all ages, success stories have shown that race, gender, religion and national origin do not matter in terms of learning potential. Why then do so many children in America have trouble in school?

Why can't all children read properly or do math? Why are so many considered "learning disabled"? Why do whole groups of children struggle, such as African-American and Latino? Why do schools, especially the public ones, seem inept and bottomless pits for money? Judging from media reports you would think that American education is a disaster with few or no answers for these questions. Yet, the truth about American education is much different and more complex than headlines indicate.

This country's important political, military and economic status is due in part to natural resources, the skills that immigrants have brought to America and the political system. However, the educational system has played a significant part, also. Many millions of past and present leaders, artists, professionals and skilled workers learned the three Rs and more in the system so maligned in recent years. Our universal school system that requires all boys and girls to attend has been copied abroad. Places in our graduate schools are highly valued by foreign students.

On the other hand, the lower schools sometimes seem much too easy for students from abroad. American adults win their share of Nobel Prizes but science and math scores of elementary and secondary students lag behind many other countries. These contradictions are a puzzle. Do successful Americans make it *in spite* of the educational system? Whole groups of people who feel abandoned (like those in big cities) might say so. Perhaps, though, our educational system is a paradox: highly successful but seriously flawed.

Homegrown critics find it easy to spot the symptoms of a deeply troubled system. Unfortunately, most critics fixate on the symptoms because they lack the knowledge and perspective to get to the heart of the matter. Such well-intentioned but misdirected concern is an old, old story.

People have complained about American education since colonial days. Today's major complaints are strikingly similar to those of the last century and the century before that. In hindsight, early complaints were to be expected. After all, formal education originally was not based on scientific study of children but on hunches, whims and self-interests. Today, however, one must wonder why so much has not changed. All other professions have changed dramatically. True, many attempts over the years have been made to reform American schools and currently the country is several years into still another attempt. In all cases, though, the reform movements have fallen far short of comprehensive overhaul. Today's schools still are based largely on the faulty knowledge of the past. Yet, incredibly, the knowledge to turn schools around has been readily available for decades.

In the last century much was learned about how children grow and how this is directly related to learning. In recent decades exciting teaching techniques have been developed that mesh perfectly with this vital knowledge of child development. Thus, there are powerful teaching tools available to all teachers. As a result there is the best of news. As long as adults do their part, 99.9% of all children can do well in school. There also is the worst of news. Few adults know or are paying attention to what has been learned, educators included. Thus, the current "reform movement" is closer to colonial thinking than to that of the twenty-first century.

The first step to true reform is to know the past. When America's educational history is examined it is clear that much of what has been done over the years never has worked well. The most devastating mistake made in the past is still being committed today: skills are often introduced too early for students to learn. Even when the timing is correct, the students are not given sufficient time to learn. Common sense dictates that if such harmful practices are recognized, they can and will be removed from schools. More opportunity then will be available to expand and refine what does work well and to add new, more effective practices. From the beginning, however, common sense is one thing that has been used too little in education.

∽

Skills are introduced too early.
Students are not given time to learn.

As typical of all classes, my second-grade students were at various reading levels. Some of the students had just begun to read. Then there was Barbara. She not only was at the top but was far above the others. Unfortunately, I was new to the school and there were no materials in the class to use with her. I went to Mrs. Jones, the teacher in the grade level above me, and asked to borrow a harder reading book. The teacher smiled and complied. After school the principal walked into my room. He told me that Mrs. Jones had complained by stating "If Barbara reads my reading book this year, what will I do with her next year?" I was dumfounded by this rigidity but realized in time that it was encouraged and even demanded by the system.

∼

"I want Chuckie to go on to second grade in September," said the adamant father.

I knew the kindergarten teacher had previously warned the parents that Chuckie would struggle greatly or even fail if he went to first grade too soon. The father, though, had been quite clear. The month of June was for promotion. His son *would* go on to first grade.

The following year I and the remedial teachers used every trick in the book but, still, the boy struggled badly. I explained to the parents that the kindergarten teacher's assessment had been correct: Chuckie simply needed more time to grow up. This would give him the best chance to succeed in second grade.

"He's going to second grade in September," said the father. "I want my son to have the chance to fail."

2

The Good Ol' Days
An Honest Look at the Past

> *"The wisest among us are engrossed in what the adult needs to know and fail to consider what children are able to comprehend...."*
> — Jean-Jacques Rousseau
> French Philosopher
> (1712–1778)

NOSTALGIA CAN BE DECEIVING. Too many adults believe that in the past most American children went to school and cheerfully learned their lessons well. Not so. At first only the children of the rich and powerful were educated. The goal of this earliest education was to prepare these students to be leaders. Instruction usually was tutorial (one teacher for a very few students) and passing state tests or earning a diploma was not an issue. This was fortunate since the quality of each tutor varied greatly. However, since most people were illiterate, anything learned by the children of the elite gave them quite an advantage.

As time went by the demand for education slowly began to increase beyond the elite. Children were brought together in larger groups to receive instruction that was geared more towards moral character than the ABCs. Often the teachers were religious leaders. If they were moral and literate, these were qualifications enough.

The idea of education for all developed very slowly. America has its roots in the ideas of independence and physical labor. Thus, many male adults (in a male-dominated society) considered "book learning" inferior to learning on the job. Other males did not believe that the poor could learn. Some viewed educated people as a threat. Consequently, when universal education was first proposed it was poorly supported. Pay and facilities were minimal. Duties for teachers included janitorial work, and severe restrictions were placed on their personal lives. Contrary views and the slightest infractions by teachers meant instant dismissal. Only two qualifications were necessary to get a job: good moral character and availability (that is, being in desperate need of a paycheck). Women, single or widowed and with few job opportunities, quickly became the bulk of the teaching workforce.

As the 1800s progressed, complaints that students were not learning became common and chronic. Many would-be reformers of education surfaced. In most cases they came from occupations such as medicine, law and religion—not from education. It was clear to these reformers that the students were not the ones responsible for their poor performance. They noted that teachers were not trained for their jobs, curriculum was primitive, and logistical support was almost nonexistent. For example, a spelling book called the *Webster's Blueback Speller* dominated the classrooms for decades. Sometimes the *Blueback Speller* was the only book in the school. A student would study and recite from that one book day after day, year after year. If a student did not show enthusiasm or skill for the repetitive and dull lessons, the teacher was free to embarrass using ridicule and to hurt using the rod.

The harmful results of such treatment of students were typified by what Horace Mann witnessed in Massachusetts. Mann was a rare combination of reformer *and* educator. While personally evaluating the many elementary schools in the state (which usually went to eighth grade) he was struck by the disorder, insubordination and violence that was routine in the schools. The violence was not always directed at or among students. Older boys were known to throw abusive, incompetent or unpopular male teachers or the principal out the school door!

Unfortunately, each reformer's effort had limited success for many reasons, such as the power of local control, a limited communication system and a lack of unity among reformers. Little did reformers know that a force much greater than their efforts would soon affect American education and that was the Industrial Revolution.

As American workers moved from farm to the dangerous mills, factories and mines, it was common for children as young as five or six to work side by side with the adults. Child advocates saw required universal education as a means to rescue the endangered children. As the century turned, more and more states passed labor and education laws that moved the children from the workplace to the classroom. Tragically, the Industrial Revolution followed the children right into the classroom.

Leaders in government and education were greatly impressed by how efficiently the factories handled the masses of raw materials to create finished products. As the population soared (fueled especially by millions of immigrants), leaders thought that industrial methods would be perfect for handling the masses of students.

Schools were modeled after the assembly line. Each grade was a work station, each teacher a worker and each student a piece of material to be molded or assembled. Each worker had a limited time to force change on the raw material before moving the material down the line. Immediately, serious problems began to surface as significant numbers of children did not do well with this "scientific management" approach. Many students struggled and even failed a grade as they were unable to meet the standards of their particular work station by the end of the school year. Eventually, they dropped out of school and performed the many labor intensive jobs then available in society. Even among the students who were successful, there were those who found the experience highly stressful and distasteful.

The response by adults in power was generally the same. Attempts were made to tinker with the system. More books and supplies were bought for the schools. Facilities were enlarged and improved. Remedial reading was instituted. Workbooks were added to supplement textbooks. Textbooks were revised or new ones adopted. Central to the thinking of adults, however, was that the system was basically sound. They noted that many students did satisfactory work and that some excelled. Therefore, any student who did poorly was lazy or, more likely, was a dunce and could not hope to do better.

Reformers who called for a change in the *basic system* were ignored. They were too few in number, did not have high enough status and, besides, the emerging school system was part of a surging and irresistible national optimism. Few were willing to listen to critics. This defeat set a pattern for the future.

Attempts to move away from the assembly-line structure in the next hundred years or so were many but always fruitless. Therefore, it is not surprising that the same problems that were present in early schools are still in today's schools. Ironically, while America now recognizes the destructive effects on adults of the workplace assembly line, we fail to recognize how destructive the same system is to those who are the most important of all, our children.

∼

Schools are modeled after the assembly line.

It was January of third grade. Billy and Joseph were nine and a half years old and they still couldn't read even the easiest of words. After two years of providing remedial help, the veteran reading teacher was discouraged and I was getting worried. Then it happened, almost like a switch being turned on. Simultaneously both boys began to read. I remember thinking that at best we adults could take only minimal credit for this change of events but I didn't know why.

∼

I watched and shook my head in dismay as the "remedial penmanship" teacher gave a lesson to my first-grade students. This district-wide mandate made no sense. Some students were already showing great skill with the pencil and didn't need the lesson. On the other hand, others barely could grasp the pencil, a condition I knew would gradually improve over time. The anguished faces of those struggling showed clearly the near impossibility of the weekly lesson.

The penmanship teacher as usual had given all students fatter "primary" pencils and rubber grips as crutches to do better. She also had given out specially lined paper. The top line had a red light next to it, the middle line, a yellow and the bottom, a green. This was supposed to help the students form and place their letters. As the outside "expert" vainly labored to keep all students interested and productive, I looked at the clock. Only ten more minutes, I thought gratefully, and the kids can go back to learning in a natural way.

3

The Nature of Kids
Child Development Research

> *"No learning ought to be learned with bondage... any learning learned by compulsion tarrieth not long in the mind."*
>
> — Plato
> Greek Philosopher and Teacher
> (427?–347 BC)

AS EDUCATION DEVELOPED in America, there was no research to guide the adults. Tutoring, colleges and then, eventually, schools for all children were instead based on experience from overseas and abundant confidence in adult common sense. The concept of research was a novel idea in society. Thus, the need for educational research was not even considered. However, by the late 1800s interest in the areas of human growth, learning and psychology began to spark investigations that were directly applicable to America's schools. By the early 1900s several theories of child development had been proposed by various researchers. Although many theories had bits and pieces that would be useful to those working in American education, three of the most notable theories came from John Dewey (1859–1952), Jean Piaget (1896–1980) and Arnold Gesell (1880–1961).

All three researchers worked in directions that were opposite to the policies present in education. Dewey viewed the classroom as a place in which children's learning could be stimulated if the learning environment was in harmony with nature (for example, if students were active, not passive). Piaget identified sequential stages of intellectual development common to all children. As each stage is reached (and not before), the child is then able to do certain intellectual tasks. Gesell also identified stages but looked at the whole child. He believed that physical, social and emotional growth was as important as intellectual growth.

The educational implication of such theories was that as a general rule adults could not simply *demand* that a student learn a skill. Struggle or failure would occur if the curriculum and classroom were organized arbitrarily or if a student lacked the developmental maturity to learn the skill being taught. Also implied was that the necessary maturity might be encouraged but could not be forced by any means, including drill, threat or physical violence.

In the western world the fact that humans were bound by laws of nature would not have been received well by those in power. Adult males deluded themselves as being apart and in control of nature. On the other hand, if questioned about the revolutionary educational theories, mothers would have smiled and replied, "So what else is new?" Every day they witnessed not only the stages of growth in their children but the individual nature of each child. Sitting up, walking, talking, and so on, were usually accomplished at different times by each sibling. None of these activities could be forced although much encouragement was given. It would seem that the mothers' experience was wasted since they had little or no voice in educational policy. At the collegiate level, however, there were some who were trying to get the word out.

As the twentieth century progressed, teacher preparation programs added the study of child development theories. Dewey's educational ideas were the first to gain a large following among professors who trained teachers. Later (and continuing today), Piaget replaced Dewey as the favorite of the professors. In the 1960s and '70s some elementary teachers tried to restructure their teaching to reflect Piaget. These efforts failed for two reasons. First, none of the power brokers in society saw a need to replace the assembly-line structure. Teachers attempting reform worked in isolation and were unsupported and even opposed by their superiors.

Second, Piaget's theory is not complete enough to use as a main force in education. Therefore, teachers had difficulty making the transition from theory to practical application.

On the other hand, Gesell's theory is much more comprehensive and is very applicable to the classroom. Gesell also had an organization formed by his subordinates to continue and make known his work. Reformers, especially in the elementary primary grades, eventually took notice and advantage of this. Their efforts resulted in dramatic school success for many children in city, suburban and country schools. Tragically and ironically, the reformers' success was destined to be ignored by society and brought the reformers a mountain of grief.

∼

Children cannot be forced to learn.

Kent was no secret to his first-grade teacher. Developmental testing and his everyday actions showed that he was normal but developmentally a year younger than what his birth certificate said and the curriculums demanded. By June Kent was not even close to second grade in many ways and, reluctantly, the parents agreed to have Kent try first grade again *if* he could have another teacher. The following year in my room Kent blossomed. For years after, the parents stopped by my house to drop off pies and cakes in gratitude. I tried more than once to explain how little I was responsible for the effects of Kent growing more mature but they emphatically brushed that argument aside and gave me all the credit.

∼

At the request of Jasmine's teacher I had observed and worked with the fourth-grade student. As I went through Jasmine's file in the office, it looked like so many others: constant struggle from the beginning of the first grade and ongoing reliance on remedial help. No wonder the teacher is worried about her attitude, I thought. Yet, Jasmine is obviously intelligent. With her skills, if Jasmine were in third grade she would fit like a hand in a glove.

4

A Call to Arms
The Developmental Reform Movement

IT IS VERY FRUSTRATING to be right and be ignored. Perhaps it is worse to be right and be maligned. Such has been Dr. Gesell's fate. The late Dr. Louise Bates Ames, one of Gesell's most trusted subordinates, once said to me that Gesell was considered a heretic by many of his contemporaries for not basing his research and clinical work on the ideas of Freud. If so, perhaps it was this friction that resulted in considerable misrepresentation of his child-development theory. Among other things, he was (and is) accused of not respecting the effect that environment has on children. Such a charge is silly for someone whose extensive educational background included a medical degree. Indeed, as early as 1929 he publicly wrote that nature and nurture must be considered together.

The idea that adults do not have total control over children did not sit well with many in psychology and higher education. Since then, prejudice against Gesell by professors in these two fields has been strong and has been passed down over the years. His theory is given short shrift in classes, if it is mentioned at all. College texts (often written by college professors) when mentioning Gesell, also reflect this prejudice. Truth be told, Gesell had more positive effect in public and private schools in the last half of the twentieth century than anyone else.

In 1951 the former subordinates of Gesell (themselves extremely talented) created what is now called the Gesell Institute of Human Development in New Haven, Connecticut. Parents sought help from the Institute for children who were having difficulties, including difficulties that were school related. The Institute's staff found that many of the school problems were caused simply by the students being in too high a grade. Eventually, observation in schools by the researchers led to the discovery that this problem of "overplacement" was not just an occasional mistake, but was extensive.

This was a stunning discovery. Adults were to blame for many a student's poor achievement! Unfortunately, this news created barely a ripple. Only gradually did the gist of the discovery spread and even then essentially only to educators and parents at the elementary level. Typically, the effort to inform was spearheaded by one or two primary teachers, sometimes aided by a courageous elementary principal and only rarely by a higher official.

The primary teachers took the lead because the higher-grade teachers had a handicap. The denser curriculum and larger number of students per day in the higher grades made it more difficult for those teachers to focus on the students as individuals. On the other hand, the primary teachers were able to see more easily the developmental stages and the individual rates of growth of the students. They also witnessed every day the tragic failure of very young children, many quite intelligent and some with the highest intelligence. The teachers' quest for change became almost personal.

These reformers did not attempt to change the entire school system. Rather, they tried to modify the faulty structure. Children who were supposed to enter school for the first time were developmentally evaluated. The standards and developmental examination most frequently used were from the Gesell Institute. Some schools used other commercial tools (that sometimes plagiarized portions of the Gesell examination) or made their own. If a child tested less than kindergarten (or first grade for schools without kindergarten), the parents were encouraged to let the child stay home for another year. This was a logical request since most mothers worked at home at that time. When mothers began to work outside the home, many schools bowed to changing times and added a grade before or after kindergarten. Regardless of method, the point was to ensure that students did not start the first grade "work station" on the assembly line too soon.

Still later, some elementary schools showed a preference for adding extra time later in the school career. Even adding an extra year between sixth and seventh grade was done. Although some adults reacted to the idea of extra time as new, the concept in our country actually is very old. It is also tried and true. Many years ago when few attended college, it was normal for some high school graduates (usually men) to do one or two extra years at private preparatory schools. These students would grow academically, physically, socially and emotionally up to what would be expected of them in college.

The practice of extra time continues today in many forms because it works. For example, the service academies are known for scholarship. When they identify prospective leaders who are not yet qualified for academy entrance, they support prep schools for these "diamonds in the rough."

Another example: There are private high schools that have added an extra year for graduates who find themselves not ready for the many demands of college or work.

The value of extra time was punctuated decades ago on campus. When the veterans of World War II "invaded" the campus using the GI Bill, they brought with them a maturity and focus that pleasantly surprised the professors and gladdened the campus police. Today, various colleges support and even encourage high school seniors to hop off the assembly line for a year or two. After a stint of real-world experience, these students enter and participate in college with an attitude and focus that all students should have.

By the 1970s the idea of extra time at the elementary level was making significant progress from New England to California. Those schools that received training from the Gesell Institute generally had the most success. Many students who would have entered first grade too soon instead had successful school careers right from the start. The earliest adopting schools saw their extra-time students graduate strongly from high school.

Some schools were much less successful or failed outright. Educators in such schools latched onto the idea of extra time without knowing fully (or at all) the underlying developmental principles. They were not able to correctly select students, develop a curriculum, do the massive public relations work necessary and trouble-shoot the inevitable problems of change. In the long run these well-intentioned but ignorant educators helped cripple the developmental movement. Their schools were used as examples by those who surfaced to oppose the developmental approach.

∼

Being in too high a grade creates academic and psychological problems.

For several years the primary teachers at the school had worked at assigning students to classrooms according to developmental levels. Flexible time also had been built into the academic program to further allow for individual differences among students. Then the principal read reports from outsiders and went to conferences that said what we were doing was wrong.

"But," some teachers said at a staff meeting, "our children are academically and socially successful and eager to come to school."

"The research says what we're doing is wrong," the principal responded stubbornly.

"Why don't we study the research and discuss it as a staff?" I suggested.

The principal went on to other business.

∼

"I understand your school has been using the developmental approach for about fifteen years," I said to the teacher in a large New Hampshire district.

"We used to," she replied. "but we don't do that anymore."

"Why not?" I asked. "Wasn't it successful?"

"Oh, it was very successful," she replied.

"I don't understand. Why stop the program?"

"Well, our principal didn't want to do it anymore," she replied in a voice filled with sadness.

"Why not, if it was working well?"

"Well, he just didn't," she said in a weak and defensive voice.

5

The "Experts" Strike Back
Infighting Among Educators

> *"Lord God, how many good and clean wits of children be now-a-days perished by ignorant schoolmasters...."*
>
> — Sir Thomas Elyot
> English Diplomat and Scholar
> (1490?–1546)

THE DEVELOPMENTAL REFORMERS tinkered with the system rather than going for total reform for many reasons. They were subject to dismissal if they challenged the system. Elementary teachers and, to a lesser extent, elementary principals did not enjoy high status in the general society or even their own profession. They were not considered experts by the public, nor were they sought out for advice on national educational issues. School educators did not make themselves known by publishing in the mass market or educational publications.

To make matters worse, there was no one national organization (like a prestigious university) to champion the cause, nor any universally read professional publication to provide information or debate. The Gesell Institute had a national audience but was not forceful when putting forth its views. Reformers working in the schools probably did not know all these specifics but had a general sense of their weak power base and peril. They pushed ahead anyway for the children.

The reformers ran into common problems. One was the many unsuccessful reforms like "new math" and "open classrooms" that swirled about the educational community in the 1960s and '70s. Each failure left the public and educational leaders a little bit more wary of future reforms. The biggest problem by far, however, was the clash of structures within the elementary school. As students stayed home for an extra year or spent that extra year in a "transition" class (the names varied greatly), this was at odds with the rest of the school and school system.While some primary teachers were successfully modifying the school structure, others within the same building who were not involved often were ignorant of the concept, confused, ambivalent or even opposed to the idea. Such lack of unity was a constant threat to the process. Yet, when extra time was implemented correctly, educators and parents deeply involved saw excellent results from the start. Struggling, unhappy students became happy achievers. Better yet, as new students enrolled, new problems were avoided.

Unknown to the developmental reformers, there were adults outside the school aghast at the idea of extra time. From past research, it seemed clear to them that students who did poorly in a grade and were "left back" (that is, failed) suffered damage. These concerned adults assumed that the developmental approach was failure in grade with another name. In 1985 a negative study on extra-time kindergarten classes in Boulder, Colorado, was published. This study became a spark for those who opposed this increasingly popular solution to failing children.

The Boulder study and others that followed tried to measure the effectiveness of the developmental approach by using standardized tests and, also, past research about failing a grade. Almost always, the conclusions were negative.

Additional critics emerged who accused developmental testing as being racially biased. They charged that far too many African-American children tested immature for such testing to be accurate. Still more critics attacked the research methods associated with the Gesell developmental examination. They said the research was based on too many advantaged white children for it to be valid for all children. What they failed to realize was that the examination simply showed a known truth: children living with poverty and other stresses mature more slowly. While good research usually requires large random groups, Gesell and his cohorts were looking for common aspects of children, not differences. They succeeded.

Despite what they saw daily in the classroom, supporters of the developmental approach were near helpless under the onslaught of negative studies and publicity. They had little of their own research to fight back with since schools as a rule did not conduct research of any kind. Superintendents and central office staffs, who should have led evaluations of the developmental approach, had not. The few positive studies that had been done were not well known nationwide and were not constructed much better than the negative studies.

The reformers also did not have the skills to effectively use anecdotal proof to support their efforts. They made little use of the local media and used the national media not at all. Even the Gesell Institute was of minimal help as it tried to respond with a low-key professional approach that was overwhelmed by aggressive and sometimes arrogant opponents.

Proponents of the developmental approach were also hindered by inherent weaknesses found among district- and school-level educators. When educational research is published, many educational leaders tend to accept the conclusions without hesitation. This is due to their lack of experience with children, especially the very young, their failure to visit the classroom and their lack of respect for their own staff.

Being closer to the action (and the truth), teachers sometimes disagree with research conclusions but do not make this known to their superiors or the public. Virtually no educators at the preK-12 level read entire research papers and discuss them with others. This consistent and irresponsible habit to skip to the bottom line masked the fact that the negative studies on the developmental approach had severe design flaws that made them invalid.

The construction of the studies indicated a lack of understanding of biology in general and, specifically, the philosophy of the developmental approach. For example, in the negative studies the *whole* child was not evaluated. Normal practice was to attempt to document gains in reading and math but, in most cases, only on a short-term basis. Standardized tests were the preferred method of measurement. (Does this sound familiar?) A few studies made attempts to measure the emotional growth of the students but these attempts were haphazard at best.

Researchers often went under the false assumption that extra time was supposed to create students who were superior to those who did not receive extra time. In reality, the true idea was to give each child the opportunity to reach full potential. Particularly crucial was the following universal flaw: no attempt was made to determine if the classrooms studied were organized according to *developmental principles.* When created correctly, an extra-time classroom has a normal curriculum, normal teacher and normal students. Yet the least knowledgeable schools often used such classrooms as dumping grounds for those with learning disabilities and/or disciplinary problems. Violations such as this were *not* recognized and discussed in the negative studies.

As parents and local educational leaders had questions, they sometimes did not have enough faith in the local educators implementing the developmental approach. It was common for them to contact colleges and state departments of education for answers. Some state departments and an occasional professor were supportive of the changes. Many, however, used the old negative research on failing a grade and the newer negative research on extra time as a guide to their advice. Considerable one-to-one public-relations efforts were needed by local schools to counteract the advice of the many well-intentioned but misinformed "experts." This was true even in schools that obviously were successful or becoming so.

The developmental approach found itself constantly in danger of being suddenly swept away by the whim of a principal, superintendent or school board. It did not take much controversy over the developmental approach to spook those in power. And when frightened or in doubt, the leaders all too often abandoned their own staff and unilaterally disbanded the program—even in schools where the program had been in place and successful for many years.

Elementary schools with the developmental approach had not recognized the need to communicate with other schools, much less document their own success. No national or state agency followed the progress of the developmental movement. The bold schools that were able to hang on existed with little support, much like tiny islands in a storm.

∼

Leaders in education tend to accept research without question.

The elementary principal had been on the job only a few months but already was getting pressure to increase test scores. Without consulting teachers, he canceled recess. This would allow for more "time on task," educational jargon for more working in seats.

∼

The expensive reading and math workbooks obviously were not developmentally appropriate for most of the kindergarteners. But the superintendent of schools had mandated that all kindergartens buy and use the workbooks and so it was done. Day after day, even those students who could barely grasp a pencil and didn't know a letter from a number struggled to fill out page after page after page.

6

Sirens of the Deep
False Cures of the Past

IN HINDSIGHT, THE BATTLE over the developmental approach created the best opportunity yet to reform American schools. Unfortunately, two strong and unrecognized factors worked against the modern reformers: the economy and the leaders. In the 1970s and '80s there was a perception that the quality of American business and industry was slipping. More and more foreign products were being bought by Americans and an exodus of American companies to less expensive parts of the world was increasing. Improving education was seen as a solution to business woes and one key to this improvement would be to spend more money.

New and bigger schools were constructed. Improvements to school libraries, more technology, additional staff, increased salaries, and in-service training all were the results of the increased funding. Yet, despite the spending of billions of tax dollars, the familiar complaints about poor student achievement continued unabated. This failure should not have been a surprise. The panacea of money had been tried many times before in the history of American education.

Meanwhile, despite the ongoing national criticism, adults associated with developmental elementary schools knew that they were on to something. There was less failure and struggle among their students. The earliest students to have the benefit of a developmental approach were entering and finishing secondary schools with good work habits and skills and an upbeat attitude. Unfortunately, these schools were but a tiny fraction of the country's total and were easy to overlook in the sea of complaints. There was no person or organization that was able to bring this small but significant core of success to the attention of the general public. This was unfortunate if only from a financial point of view. Providing extra time to learn costs far less than school remediation efforts and the results of school failure: poverty and crime. As inflation soared and school budgets increased year after year (especially in special education), taxpayers revolted by cutting and limiting school funding.

As developmentalists tinkered with school structure, other reformers tinkered with educational nuts and bolts. New report cards were designed to try to eliminate the stigma of Ds and Fs. Social promotion was instituted for the same reason. School space was redesigned as "open classrooms." Some frustrated reformers even created private alternative schools. None of these ideas were comprehensive enough to make a difference. Many of the changes were mandated from above and not always supported by the teachers. Their sole result was to give the public the impression that educators flitted from one fad to another and did not know what they were doing. In response to wasted money and seemingly unfocused educators, a second age-old panacea was resurrected: effort.

For the past several years the push to "get tough" on students (and teachers) has been led by adults outside of education. Officials in business and industry, state governors, federal senators, congressmen and even the president of the United States have cried out for "raising the bar." The point of using this sports metaphor, of course, is to emphasize that each student needs to strive to improve. However, athletes in the pole vault or high jump have much control over their goals (the height of the bar). Students, especially early on, not only have their goals forced upon them but also the timelines and methods of "training."

For the most part, educational leaders have been reacting to this pressure with uninspired, discredited and destructive solutions. Academic requirements have been pushed lower in the grades. ("If the kids can't learn to read at age six, let's start them at age five or even four!") Longer school days and years have been adopted by some systems. Homework has been mandated as low as kindergarten. In some schools so much homework is assigned that students do not have time at home to do invaluable enrichment activities such as scouting, hobbies, physical play, and so on. The irony of the increased homework is that much, perhaps most, of the homework is uninspired and accomplishes a lot less than the public thinks.

Most recently, there has been a push for every school system in every state to teach the same thing (that is, reach the same goals). Standardized testing of curriculums has become an obsession. Passing or failing a grade and getting a diploma based only on such tests has been instituted. So desperate have some school leaders become to improve test scores, they have reduced or eliminated art, music, physical education ... and even recess.

Such leadership responses reflect the forced nature of the assembly-line structure and a lack of knowledge about children. All organizations do need a minimum of funds to operate and students should be challenged. And in the past increased money and pressure improved school facilities and fostered some academic improvement in some students. Typically, though, the amount of improvement did not justify the expense and tension. Also, many of the improved conditions and results were not permanent. This failure of money and effort was created by the inherent flaws of these panaceas.

For money to be effective, it must be spent on the things that really work and count the most. The history of educational funding has largely been to spend more on what's been done in the past, regardless of its effectiveness. To make matters worse, increased funding is eventually redirected, reduced or eliminated as normal or unexpected national or world events shape decisions. The present reform movement is only the most recent illustration of the funding roller coaster.

After the mania of the '90s stock market rise, the chaos of the "dot com" collapse followed. Immediately, the federal government and most state governments went deeply into debt. Suddenly, most (if not all) public school districts faced deep cuts in support. Then, the war on terrorism began, demanding many billions of dollars earmarked or available for other uses. Although political leaders still pledge increased support for education, where is the money to come from, not only for past funding levels, but for the new expensive state and federal mandates?

The old panacea of increased effort (pressure) is just as flawed. Results gained under pressure often do not last because it is like cramming for a test. Much is forgotten immediately after the test. In essence, our assembly-line education with so many students in over their heads is nonstop cramming. One hint of this is when teachers lament in September about the "forgetting" that is done by students over the summer vacation. While critics offer a shorter summer vacation as a solution, everybody misses the real point. That which is forgotten over any vacation never was learned in the first place.

Some school critics are pleased that improvement is being made on state and federal mandated tests. What is being overlooked, however, is that great effort is being spent by many simply to gain a minimum standard. Learning for humans should not be that difficult.

The effort panacea depends on the energy of everyone involved, both adults and students. Over time, the effort to force more learning into the students cannot be maintained as both the adults and students start to wear down. At school this wearing down is being reflected in the adults by an increase in teacher absences, career changes and, when financially possible, early retirements. Students are showing this wear and tear in their psychological well-being and incorrect behaviors such as cheating and substance abuse.

As educational leaders focus only on demands from above and without, their latest recycling of past panaceas has been damaging to public relations. Teachers as a group are seen (unfairly) as inept and administrators as having been lax, at best, and not being in charge, at worst. This pattern of educational leaders holding on to the past and possessing no creative and valid vision has been a chronic characteristic of American education. If our educational system is viewed as a ship being tossed about the stormy waters of society, few educational captains have ever emerged to see where port is, much less sail strong and true against the wind.

∽

More money and effort are not panaceas.

Discipline had deteriorated in the upper elementary wing to the point that one class was openly defying the teachers and I no longer allowed my primary students to enter the wing. One of the teachers of the offending students, in an effort to squelch the rebellion, arranged a meeting among the parents of the child ringleader, the principal and the teacher. One of the parents was known to be difficult when sober and worse when under the influence of alcohol. At the appointed time all the participants walked into the conference room. Quickly, the principal grabbed an empty coffee cup and left the room, never to return. After a very long and awkward wait, the parents and teacher conducted a meeting that desperately needed the school leader.

∼

The third-grade children were not sitting down in rows listening to me lecture. Rather, at this particular time they were doing individual assignments in reading, writing, math and art. There was movement and low talking as the students worked on projects, got up to use a class resource or ask me a question. A candidate for the principalship came to observe the school's classrooms. He took one step into my room and froze. A look of sheer horror showed on his face as he took in the unfamiliar scene. I wanted to talk to him to explain the class routine but quickly he left the room. The candidate got the job.

7

Few Caesars to Be Found
The Sorry State of Educational Leadership

> *"... as the schoolmaster is, so will be the school."*
> — Anonymous
> Quoted by John Stuart Mill
> English Economist and
> Philosopher (1806–1873)

AN OBVIOUS QUESTION MUST be asked. If the developmental approach was so successful, why didn't all educational leaders support the practice and lead the charge? The answer lies in a "secret" that rarely sees the light of day. When veteran teachers consider the principals, superintendents and other supervisors that they have worked under, the teachers rank many of them as inferior or incompetent. When teachers are talking among themselves they have been known to state, "He's a good boss. He leaves me alone." This damning with faint praise is usually reserved for a boss who may be a nice guy and a lover of kids but is barely adequate, or even inept. Evaluations of lesser leaders are less charitable and would startle citizens who assume a school or system to be in good hands.

Teachers' low evaluations of their leaders is nothing new. In fact, it should be expected since inferior educational leadership is as old as complaints about the students' performance. Partial proof of this ineptness is the historical trend of educational leaders to react to outside pressure rather than initiate reform themselves. In times of calm they flit from educational fad to educational fad. In times of national reform they adopt whatever panacea is being pushed at large and, thus, is politically safe.

Partly to blame for the poor leadership of the past is that schools were not subject to the forces of the open market. Unlike business or industry, schools did not compete, either against each other or a standard. Even the earliest settlers intuitively believed in a concept that would later be called the bell curve. The bell curve indicates that only a few people are born superior. Most are average and some are born inferior. Thus, superior performance from all students was not expected.

Since schools were not subject to comparison, neither were their leaders. In fact, until recently, schools and school systems existed in isolation. State and local school boards did not witness the day-to-day operations of their schools. True and total control was left to superintendents and principals. This might not have been a bad thing if the selection process for educational leaders had been satisfactory.

The move to universal education was overshadowed by great changes in our society. Talented men who were not farmers were drawn into engineering, medicine, law and other emerging professions but not that often into the less prestigious classroom. Although women were allowed to work in schools, society expected them to eventually get married and work at home. Thus, the pool for career teachers of both genders was limited. Since school leaders usually came from within, the pool for educational leaders was even more limited.

At best, the selection of leaders was based on primitive measures. Teachers were judged by their ability to keep their classes quiet and busy, rather than by student learning. When a teacher applied to be principal and, later, to higher positions, a reputation of keeping order was of great help in being selected. This high emphasis on controlling the "masses" is easily seen in an unspoken relationship between our schools and sports. For many decades, coaches had (and perhaps still have) an edge when applying for elementary and secondary leadership positions. Not only were coaches highly visible in the community, they were perceived as good controllers of students and subordinates.

Politics, of course, also played a major part. School positions were a steady source of patronage. If the selection process seemed scandalously deficient, it must be remembered that schools below the college level were of minor concern to those in power. What was most important happened in the workplace.

The selection process was also affected by the upbeat nature of American society and the sense of superiority of adults. Adults were creating great change in many facets of society. The "paltry" problems related to school children surely could be met by the adult, any adult, in charge. Poor or failing grades and retention simply was an official acknowledgement of student inferiority. This contradictory attitude—adults know best and are in control but blame the children when things go wrong—enabled educational leaders to retain their positions and be promoted regardless of how students performed. Wars, the Depression and other crises in America generated much debate on curriculum reform and funding but never on the abilities of the educational leaders. For example, the launching of Sputnik in 1957 created a hue and cry for more teaching of math and science and, of course, more money, but not for an evaluation of principals, superintendents and college professors.

The faulty selection process was aggravated by the motivation of many who applied for the leadership positions. After just a few years of poorly paid teaching, men frequently sought a principalship for the sole reason of wanting to make enough money to support a family. Others, especially men, were lured to the leadership positions for the power and (as long as they did not rock the boat) the ability to administer this power largely independent of oversight. Still others applied because they did not like teaching, were not good at it and found it easier and safer to drift upwards in education than to compete in other occupations.

No amount of teaching guarantees a good leader but logic indicates significant knowledge of children is a prerequisite for making correct decisions. Since many principal positions required only three years of teaching, this encouraged the running of schools and school systems by those with minimal knowledge. Today, teaching experience sometimes is not even required. Rather, knowledge of student standardized tests is the new barometer of competence.

Regardless of how and why leaders were chosen, being selected meant almost a guarantee of employment. As long as educational leaders bent to the wishes of their superiors, did not get arrested and, especially, did not propose anything revolutionary, their jobs were secure. Until now. Well, maybe.

In the last few years critics have finally begun to focus somewhat on the people at the top. While past reform movements focused on the curriculum and teachers, at first glance it appears that educational leaders are included in today's movement. However, the assumption generally is that current leaders need to (and can) improve test scores rather than that they lack competence. The stimulus for this unique, if flawed, focus on leadership may have several sources, one of which being America's change from a manufacturing economy to one of information. Not to be overlooked, however, is the changed status of the student "elite."

In the past, the above-average to superior students could be counted upon to do well in school, regardless of events in society. Over the last several years, however, there has been a perceived decline in their academic performance. This decline in the elite has shaken not only power brokers, but also many of those adults most likely to vote. Political leaders, sensing an opportunity to win votes, have jumped on this latest call for educational reform. With pressure to improve coming from all directions, educational leaders can find fewer places to hide, especially from the obsession with test scores.

The result has been a steep decline in the number of people applying for educational leadership positions. The positions are seen by many educators (who might apply) as one big headache at best, and impossible at worst. Thus, a historically weak pool of candidates is becoming even weaker.

In the past, the relatively few excellent leaders never had the critical mass to effect permanent change, either locally or nationally. They did have some freedom, however, to quietly modify some harmful dictates from above. Their position today is weaker, as state and federal governments substitute their judgment for those working closest to the children. Even the best leaders are being forced to take the false paths of more money and effort. The many unsatisfactory leaders, with minimal educational knowledge, vision and leadership skills, are used to sailing with the wind and continue to do so. And the teachers? They continue to follow orders, no matter what.

∾

Education has a history of poor leadership.

Most of the school's teachers were meeting after school to discuss what to do about the new principal. Having had the job for a year, the principal had shown a knack for making all the wrong decisions. For this trait he had been kicked downstairs to our school by the superintendent, who was overheard to say, "Those teachers are a good bunch. They'll run the school for him." Although the teachers lamented long on the situation, there was no consensus for the principal's removal. Typical was one teacher's whine, "I don't want him to lose his job." Listening to the discussion, I was reminded of the fable "The Belling of The Cat."

∼

The veteran teacher came to my room after the staff meeting.

"Rowland, what the boss is telling us to do is bad for the kids! We all know that!"

I knew what she wanted. As usual I was supposed to lead the opposition. Too often in the past, however, I had gone out on a limb, looked behind and found no one else there. This time I suggested an alternative.

"Why don't you go to the boss and tell him that? Or bring it up at the next staff meeting?"

She recoiled. "Oh, no! I can't do that," she said and left the room.

8

The Caregivers
Strengths and Weaknesses of Teachers

AS SOCIETY HAS CHANGED over the years, and reform movements have come and gone, teachers have been one constant. Although in the past many became teachers at least in part out of necessity, love of the children was and still is a prime motivator. What has changed is the preparation of the teachers. There came a time when society realized that merely being an adult was not enough to be a school teacher.

The first attempt at preparation was simply the requirement that a teacher had graduated from the local school. In rural areas this perhaps meant having completed the eighth grade and in larger towns having a high school diploma. Eventually, two-year "normal schools" were set up to train only those high school graduates who wanted to be teachers. Later, four-year college programs were set up, and for decades they reflected what was thought to be the most modern way to train teachers.

Prospective teachers took a regular undergraduate curriculum but included in that were courses aimed only at prospective teachers. Educational psychology, history of education and "methods" (how to actually teach, say, math or reading) were typical of the education courses required. Toward the end of the four-year period, the prospective teachers would then do "student (practice) teaching" in a public or private school. Theoretically, the new teachers were then qualified to be hired. The reality was much different as the preparation program was riddled with weaknesses.

Many of the professors had achieved their positions not by

being experts at what they taught but because of their paper credentials. Much of the curriculum was theoretical or irrelevant to the real classroom. As a whole, the curriculum was absurdly easy, sometimes demeaning and lacking the respect of professors and students in other disciplines. Perhaps in one sense this lack of rigor was appropriate since prospective teachers needed minimal qualifications to enter the preparation program.

In theory, all aspects of the four years of preparation came together during student teaching. The late timing of student teaching seemed logical if the preparation courses were necessary. Unfortunately, the quality of student teaching often was as poor as the preparation courses. Technically, student teaching was supervised by the college but actually was left to the preK-12 schools. Student teachers were supposed to be matched up with master teachers but, here too, the reality was different. Principals often assigned student teachers to those staff members who were willing (sometimes grudgingly) to go through "the bother" of having a student teacher. Other mentors were selected because the boss felt comfortable with them, not because the veteran teachers were topnotch or innovative. Some mentors were chosen only because no one volunteered.

Student teachers who were placed where they were not truly welcome were stuck until their student teaching was completed. There was supposed to be a close liaison between the college and the "cooperating" school. For the most part, however, the supervision of the student teacher was left solely to the cooperating school's mentor teacher. Sometimes a college contact person came to observe and talk with the student teacher (and mentor) but this was minimally helpful.

Hindering cooperation between college and cooperating school was antagonism that developed from the different educational cultures. The college culture nurtured the idea that professors were superior because of their degrees and position. PreK-12 school teachers resented this snobbishness and viewed the professors as pretenders working in a make-believe world. After all, many professors had not taught preK-12 children for many years while others had no experience at all!

Student teaching had other sticky points that proved harmful to both future teachers and their future young students. The teaching was usually done in the senior year of college. This meant that after more than three years of study, some future teachers suddenly, and shockingly, found that being with children was the last thing they desired. This meant that they either had to change majors and write off many expensive courses or after graduation take a job that they immediately or eventually would dislike.

As well, student teaching was not enough training for many. Although a few colleges required two student-teaching experiences, the total time spent in practicing the craft was at best several weeks. Unfortunately, most school districts did not have a peer mentoring system to help newly hired teachers pick up the slack in their preparation. In this sink-or-swim atmosphere, the new teachers who had excellent potential (and there were many) learned on their own on the job. The others quit after a few years of frustration or, worse, hung on as marginal or incompetent educators.

With luck obviously having a great deal to do with developing a first-rate new teacher, it might seem amazing that good teachers were produced at all. In fact, the many good teachers who inspired students can be attributed more to sex discrimination and love than to the teacher-preparation system. Until recently, the few career choices for women made it inevitable that teaching would attract its share of those talented women who worked outside the home. Also, teaching is a caregiving occupation. The love of children was a strong force in the recruitment of teachers. Even if women (and men) initially chose teaching solely to get bread on the table, the caregiving aspect encouraged the most dedicated to remain on the job.

Today, there are signs of change in teacher preparation. Colleges are being more selective of those who apply to be teachers. There is a growing awareness at the collegiate level that preparation courses need to have more meat. It is becoming recognized that those who teach preparation courses cannot isolate themselves within ivy walls and must themselves be experts.

Prospective teachers today are more likely to gain experience with children early on in their college career to see if teaching really is for them. Student teaching for many now means longer, more varied stints and better supervision by the colleges. The peer mentoring of new teachers is starting to catch on. There is a growing sense among colleges and school districts that both groups have important roles to play and cooperation is vital.

Unfortunately, these reforms are not even close to being universal and in many cases are still scratching the surface. For example, even though they have been raised, scholastic requirements to be admitted to teacher programs remain modest and are much lower than other professional programs. The programs themselves still are not respected by other disciplines as being rigorous. At the school level, a student teacher still is just as likely to get an incompetent or reluctant mentor as a master teacher. Much is like it was decades ago.

The obstacles to substantial reform of teacher preparation and education, in general, are historical, economic and sociological. The biggest obstacle, however, may be the caregiving nature of those attracted to teaching. Caregivers are not radical in thought and deed. Their nature is to nurture and soothe. Questioning or opposing authority is foreign to caregivers because disequilibrium and conflict make them very uncomfortable. They respect authority to the point of being fearful. If you want to start a revolution you do not start with caregivers.

Over the years this has meant that teachers have been unwilling or unable to demand respect and good working conditions for themselves. No matter how incompetent or abusive a boss they might have had, how low the pay or poor the working conditions, teachers have not stood up for themselves. Far more serious, however, and even unforgivable, is that their fear of criticism or retaliation has prevented them from sticking their necks out to protect the children. Since education uses top-down management, policies that make no sense to those who know children have been implemented often and unopposed.

It has been popular for several years in educational circles to talk of "empowering the teachers," that is using their expertise to improve education. Like all other educational reforms, however, giving power to teachers has been infrequently and unevenly attempted. Even when given a chance to exert control, many teachers remain leery of accepting the responsibility, be it a team leader of peers or formally evaluating their superiors. It is just not part of their being.

It is ironic that the strength of caregivers is also their greatest weakness. Perhaps they do have enough latent moral courage if not to lead the way to a child-friendly education then at least to assist the effort. If so, this quality must be nurtured at least as early as the teacher-preparation program and continued by understanding and courageous leaders. Unfortunately, the present professors and preK-12 leaders are themselves a product of our flawed educational system. Like most classroom teachers, the majority of these power brokers show little resemblance to Patrick Henry.

~

A teacher's greatest strength is linked to a great weakness.

It was the week before the start of school. The mother stood in my classroom doorway with child in hand.

"Mr. Creitz, I've just moved into town. My daughter, Anna, is supposed to go into the second grade but I don't think she's ready for that. She struggled all last year with reading and even holding a pencil was difficult. She didn't want to come to school."

I looked at the child. Shy and small with thumb stuck in her mouth, she easily could have been mistaken for a kindergartener. I suggested that I give the child a developmental examination, even though inwardly I suspected what the results would be. Sure enough, Anna showed herself to be normal but barely up to first-grade level in all areas of growth. When I agreed that Anna would do best in first grade the mother sighed with relief.

As I watched Anna operate successfully and happily in my primary room during the ensuing months, she showed clearly that she belonged. I don't remember her missing a day.

∽

Some kids in the first grade had mastered the lower case letters. Others were at the opposite end, writing many letters backward. As I tested the waters and corrected some of their letters, I knew it was too soon for them. Then there was Richard. He was typical of those who were developmentally in-between. I sensed he was ready to master all the letters. For two days I had showed him the difference between b and d but it hadn't stuck. The third day he showed me his written story with a huge grin. "I know this d is backward," he said. He pointed to the offending letter and walked away. I didn't ask him why he hadn't corrected the letter because I was laughing too hard.

9

The Child's Structure
How Biology Affects Learning

> *"Man is developed...not only by what he receives and absorbs from without, but much more by what he puts out and unfolds from himself...."*
> — Friedrich Froebel
> German Educator
> (1782–1852)

ONE OF THE COSTS OF POOR leadership and meek subordinates is that bad practices become bad habits. Bad habits then lead to mythology. One example is how, when and why children begin school. For the last hundred years state laws have dictated that young children be placed in school (specifically, first grade) by a certain chronological age. At first the laws varied and many were flexible. Some did not require school entrance until age eight. In practice, however, most children entered first grade at about age six. Perhaps this was because many children can use numbers, letters and writing tools to some extent at this age. However, as adults focused on the birth certificate, many failed to recognize the wide range of differences among the six year olds.

Some of the students were academically "advanced" (that is, reading), some were just ready to attempt the curriculum and others were not ready at all. The adults, who did notice the variation, unfortunately accepted it as proof of the bell-curve theory. The theory, however, has no place in school because most humans have an infinite capacity to learn. Thus, even a child with modest potential can learn many, many things in school if handled correctly.

To do this requires knowing that learning depends on many factors, with development being one of the most important.

Although child development can be divided into many aspects, the following four are comprehensive and most useful: physical, intellectual, social and emotional. Each part of development is crucial in itself for learning to occur. Consider the physical.

When adults think of a child's physical development they frequently consider the most visible characteristics: height and weight. For academic learning, however, physical development also involves coordination and stamina. Reading, for example, depends on a certain maturity in the small muscles of the eyes to focus on each letter and word and then move across and down text without losing one's place. For writing, maturity is also needed in the small muscles of the hand to hold the pencil, form the letters or numbers to a correct size and place the figures correctly—all at the same time! Even if children have the required muscular control to learn, they must also have developed sufficient stamina. If maturation is lacking, the students may start work with a lot of energy but tire and finish weakly or not at all.

Stresses such as poor diet, illness and abuse affect physical development and this has been widely known for years. The many children who enter school each year with a background of hardship therefore are proof positive of a need for a flexible school structure.

A student who is physically developed enough for a task will make little progress without the proper intellectual development. Reading serves as an excellent example. Assuming a child's eyes are physically mature enough to focus on letters and numbers, the brain still must differentiate between fifty-two letters (twenty-six upper and twenty-six lower case) and ten numbers. An immature student easily confuses similar figures such as b, d, p, q, 6 and 9. The auditory portion of the brain also must be mature enough. The phonetic sounds of letters and numbers are many and sometimes very similar in sound (for example, p/b/d/3/z).

The brain, of course, also must be mature enough to perceive and make sense of the many combinations of letters and numbers *and* their many exceptions. Note how the physical must mesh with the intellectual for reading to occur. Even this much of developmental reality clashes with chronological entrance into school and arbitrary grade-level expectations. The chance for school success becomes even less when other parts of development are ignored.

It is understood if even the brightest child who is a victim of poverty, neglect, illness or violence finds it difficult to concentrate on school tasks. Even a single traumatic event can have a long-term devastating effect on learning. Many school services (local, state and federal) are available to try to compensate for these destructive forces. When there is no obvious cause of school difficulty, however, confusion reigns. A few examples will illustrate such a mysterious situation.

A precocious child talks up a storm as a toddler, learns to read at age five but fails first grade. A "straight A" student with outstanding SAT scores goes to college but flunks out the first semester. Such baffling cases have occurred all too frequently as long as there have been schools. Sometimes a child does not fail outright. Instead, the child underachieves while parents and teachers scratch their heads at the less-than-stellar effort. Often the offending child is thought to be lazy, undisciplined or affected by some undiagnosed disability. Sometimes the finger of guilt points to the school. The child's teacher must be incompetent. The school's budget is insufficient. The cause in most cases, however, is none of these reasons. Rather, it is the school structure that ignores the social and emotional part of each child.

For a child to learn best, school placement and tasks must match the social and emotional levels of the child. Then, most energy can be directed towards learning. Mismatched placement and tasks cause stress. The child's energy then is used first and foremost to survive. The child may shut down and refuse to attempt school work, even if the child can do it and even if the work is easy. Sometimes the opposite happens. A precocious child may do nothing but study as a means of self-protection. The academic zeal and excellent grades hide the lack of growth in other vital areas.

There is much evidence in the everyday life of humans that proves the importance of proper social and emotional growth. The biographies of many prominent child actors demonstrate this. Pushed as early as possible into stage and screen careers by parents (and, thus, into situations beyond their maturity), not only do many child actors live unstable, lonely and unhappy lives as children, they don't recover as adults. Yet despite these well-known disasters, adults still are in a hurry as they enroll their three, four and five year olds in dance or music lessons. Then they make the rounds of talent agencies, hoping for that one chance at fame and fortune.

Unfortunately, the mismatching of developmental levels and required tasks is duplicated in less spectacular but just as devastating fashion millions of times each and every year with "ordinary" children. All across the country, school children find themselves mismatched academically, physically, socially and emotionally right from the start. As a rule this is caused simply by being enrolled based on the birth certificate and encountering the rigidity of the system. Yet schools can prevent most of this suffering if child development is taken into account.

It is possible to measure, through testing or observation, each area of development. Then, the school program can be adjusted to fit each child. For example, teaching techniques now exist to accommodate the wide range of academic levels found in any class. Thus, academically advanced students can remain comfortably with classmates who are at similar social and emotional levels. Students who are less advanced academically need not be rushed into failure as is done now. Not only can they coexist and profit from the expertise of their academically precocious buddies, the "late bloomers" also have valuable skills that they can pass on to the rest of the class. Thus, everybody wins when child development is taken into account.

While each part of child development is important in itself for learning, the pieces always interact with each other to create the whole child. Only when the school structure reflects this whole child instead of intellectual bits and pieces will children have the chance to reach their full academic potential. Only then will they stop bringing home report cards that have comments like "Jake could do better if he tried."

∼

Developmental maturity is necessary for learning.

James' high reading ability had prompted the school to mistakenly skip him a grade the year before. Now it was September in fifth grade and, although he could do the work, he was so tense he drooled. To make matters worse, James had no true friends among the older children.

The structure of my fourth/fifth grade combination class encouraged the students to mix and respect individual differences. James liked working with other students (including his younger friends), whether doing a traditional written assignment or using his hands with project materials. He spent much of his free time creating clay "masterpieces," a task that was obviously therapeutic for him.

As the fall progressed James began to relax and stopped drooling. Then his well-intentioned parents laid down the law to James and me. He was to sit in his seat all day and do paper work only. He was in the fifth grade and had to act "appropriately." James' drooling resumed and got worse.

∽

Beth and Bea, two twin "preemies" now in third grade, were keeping their heads above water, a pattern they had shown since kindergarten. Fortunately, they had entered first grade older, at age seven. That first academic year had been difficult and they probably would need ongoing extra help for years but it was obvious that neither sister could have succeeded in school at the "correct" earlier age.

10

Fooling with Mother Nature
Dangers of Forced Learning

THE PATTERN OF CHILD DEVELOPMENT generally is the same throughout the world. Consider locomotion. Children crawl, walk and run in that order. However, because of a unique genetic makeup, each child may accomplish each stage of growth in locomotion (or any other skill) at a slightly different chronological age. This variation in rates of maturation is in direct conflict with the rigid and arbitrary American school structure. To compound the problem, each area of development is affected when the growth of a child significantly deviates from the original blueprint. Consider the example of preemies.

Children born prematurely play "catch-up" for many years, at best. By school entrance the children almost always are less mature than their chronological ages—and the demands of the curriculum. The more premature any child is, the more likely the child is to have true, substantial and permanent learning disabilities when entering school. Similar negative effects on development are seen when growth is slowed or skewed by lack of food, lack of health care or poor nurturing by adults.

Each year in modern society, many students from deprived or abusive situations enter school for the first time. Many of them are not able to match the immediate expectations of the schools. Since learning depends on growth (and emotional stability), getting the academic skills and related behavior up to "grade level" quickly just is not biologically possible. Yet, because the assembly line waits for no one, considerable remedial services are used to attempt to do the impossible. Sadly, much evidence has existed for many years that this is not the way to go.

As long as biology has been a subject of interest, people have tried to manipulate mother nature. Over the years many experiments have been performed that have hothoused the growth stages in other animals and plants. Universally, the results have been dismal. Creatures that are pressured to mature quicker than normal are susceptible to severe injury and death. For those that survive, the risk then becomes one of premature aging and an early death. These destructive results can be seen outside of the laboratory. Consider society's obsession with sports.

The unfortunate rise of organized competitive and team sports for kids as young as four has come with a penalty that was unforeseen by many. The physical toll on these early players includes injuries not seen in the past until middle age. The emotional toll is far greater.

It is not unusual for those who participate very early in organized sports to abandon sports by the time they become teenagers. The requirements of the young to train hard, compete, win and be under scrutiny by teammates and adults (some poorly behaved) does not allow for natural intellectual, physical, social and emotional growth. In the schools, also, there is ample evidence that rushing children beyond their natural pace is destructive.

There has long been a saying that kids in kindergarten run to school, by third grade they walk and by sixth grade they drag their feet. It might be added that by high school many drop out or show destructive behavior. This behavior, of course, sometimes reflects difficulties not related to school. However, quite often it reflects damage to various areas of development as the structure of the school is forced upon the students. For example, social and emotional damage is created as early as first grade by the demand to read and write. For those not mature enough to be successful (yet), a false sense of inferiority is created by the struggle. Self-comparisons to other students, report cards, remedial work or being labeled as handicapped reinforces this negative image.

Intellectual damage is created as students falsely assume that they have no aptitude in certain academic areas. They also assume that, in general, learning must be a struggle and not enjoyable. Perhaps not surprising, a major cause of bullying is the emotional and intellectual damage done early on in school. Being aggressive becomes the one area in which the "failed" bullies can succeed.

Hothousing children also can result in negative physical changes. For example, children under stress often have frequent headaches and stomachaches. Elementary students often regress to younger behaviors such as bedwetting and thumb sucking. Some negative physical changes can become permanent, particularly in the area of vision.

The stereotype of a bookworm with glasses is not an accident. Experience has shown that the earlier humans do close and fine work, such as reading and writing, the more likely they will have significant and permanent visual problems later on. To make matters worse, modern society adds another heavy burden on the eyes. Watching a video screen, be it the regular TV, computer or video game, mimics the stress of reading and writing. Although the human eye has the flexibility to work at short, medium and long ranges, it can be damaged by prolonged close-up work.

Research, including that done by the Gesell Institute, indicates that children are naturally farsighted during the first few years of school. Requiring them to read and write before their eyes mature places great strain on the eyes. Yet, for at least a century students have been required to read and write in first grade, at age six, and in many schools today in kindergarten, at age five.

Primary grade teachers are all too familiar with the many children in their classes who strain to make use of the letters and numbers. Pressured by time, the teachers try to compensate by encouraging the student to use a straight edge under the line of print instead of backing off and giving a proper assignment. Writing, which necessitates mature muscles both in the eyes and hands, is even more demanding for the young child. Work that requires moving eyes from far to near and back again (such as copying work off the board) combines the difficulties of reading and writing. Such a task is impossible for many.

Sadly, many adults seem totally ignorant or uncaring of the relationship of developmental strain to underachievement, misbehavior and physical problems. In fact they are making a bad situation worse. The consumer industry and some parents encourage children to act older than they are. The resulting stress is brought right into school. Although many educators try to counter the abnormal behavior, they work against their own efforts by allowing skills to be forced lower and lower in the grades. As stress increases for children throughout society, reading, writing and computer instruction are replacing recess, the sand table and the easel even as low as kindergarten.

∽

Forcing maturation damages children.

Eunice entered my first grade with some permanent physical problems and, developmentally, was barely five overall. Fortunately, she was in a continuous-progress primary classroom that molded the curriculum to her development. Unfortunately, the state and federal "reforms" were kicking in.

The principal mandated that Eunice receive a remedial reading program that was politically in vogue because it mimicked the "get tough" philosophy of the reform movement and guaranteed results (that, not incidentally, were biologically impossible and mathematically improbable). I stated that Eunice was not ready to read and, at best, money and time would be wasted. At worst, Eunice could learn to hate reading. I was overruled. Several weeks into the program the remedial reading teacher came to me and quietly posed a question: "Would it be alright with you if Eunice was dropped from the program? She's not ready to read yet."

∼

The principal was not pleased that we first-grade teachers planned to keep one-third of our students with us another year. He could not understand how so many could not be up to grade level in the curriculums. As the pressure from him increased, we teachers guarded our share of the remedial services zealously, hoping the remedial help would be our ace in the hole. Yet, in the deepest corner of our heart of hearts, we knew the remedial services were a waste of time and money. For most of the kids there would be no miracle. Developmentally, the students were not yet mature enough for the skills demanded.

11

Mindless Momentum
Misplaced Loyalty to the System

THE WHOLESALE FAILURE OF America to recognize the lack of sync between school and how students grow and learn is a study in itself. One reason for this failure is that for many years the schools did seem to be working. The bulk of the students were learning at least some basic skills. Although many dropped out as early as age 14, even the dropouts could find unskilled work or learn skills as apprentices. There was a presumption of opportunity to work one's way up the ladder of success, even from the bottom rung. America was a country on the rise economically and politically and there was no reason to question its institutions.

When bad times happened, such as war or depression, they were not linked to the schools. Personal misfortune was blamed on inferior human character, being born to the wrong family or mere fate. Thus, for many years there was no regular, concerted and national effort to study what schools were doing. This is unfortunate since the flaws (or at least the poor results) were obvious to those who bothered to look. Would-be reformers discovered, however, that scientific management practices such as the assembly line created a resistance to change and the momentum to self-perpetuate.

One of the most destructive aspects of the assembly line is that time is a constant and limited. The line has a single speed, must avoid slowing down and, above all, must never stop. With this idea ingrained in the schools, flexibility was and still is discouraged. Of course, over the years good teachers have tried to adjust to the many variations of students in their classes but, technically, they are not supposed to do this. The students are supposed to bend to the curriculum and not vice versa. The A–F report cards, grade retention and standardized tests (particularly those geared to specific grades) all reinforce the most rigid aspects of the system.

The crusading primary teachers of the 1960s, '70s and '80s found the inexorable flow of the line to be a huge obstacle to change. Even the few parents, public officials and educators who saw the need did not have a comprehensive idea of what the change should be and how it would be implemented. Extra time at the primary level was seen as a way to begin. This measure would help some children, yet be politically feasible. However, even this modest interruption in the steady flow of the line was difficult to do. It needed constant explaining to the public. (Note: The steady flow of the educational assembly line is an illusion created by overlooking the dropouts and the uneven achievement of those who do make graduation.) Most educational leaders looked for politically safer means to improve student performance. They thought they found it in the "medical model."

The medical-model approach assumes that if a child has difficulty learning, the child is "sick." Medicine then is given to cure the problem without interfering with the line. This medicine is remedial work.

Many students need some extra help at some time or another. Even in college the brightest student might need tutoring in chemistry or Russian. However, the medical model goes far beyond the occasional helping hand. A hint of this medical model surfaced as early as the 1930s in the form of remedial reading. However, this medicine did not come close to eliminating Ds and Fs on report cards and grade retentions. The blame continued to be placed on the students.

In the mid-1960s thinking began to change. With the emphasis on the effects of poverty and discrimination, attitudes towards students doing poorly softened. These students were seen more as victims than being personally responsible. Great sums of money were available for the first time from the federal government to support new school services for those underachieving students considered to be "disadvantaged."

The medical model also received indirect support from school educators. Over the years many teachers witnessed the conflict between what they were required to do and the nature of children. By the late 1960s the absurdity of giving young children failing grades spurred change in some elementary schools. Report cards, especially at the primary level, switched numbers for letter grades. The intention was to show growth rather than competition with others and time. The change was futile as many adults and students incorrectly equated the numbers with the old A–F system.

Parent conferences were instituted to supplement or replace report cards (a good step). Gradually, social promotion was instituted, especially in the lowest grades. Contrary to popular belief, social promotion was not a lowering of standards by teachers and principals. It reflected the desperation and limited options of the educators. Under such conditions, the remedial services of the medical model appeared to be a lifeline. This lifeline, however, turned out to be a bargain with the devil.

Over the years many adverse effects of the medical model/remediation approach surfaced. Using this approach did not result in significant and lasting gains. It sparked a never-ending spiral of hiring more staff and buying more materials and equipment. In the early 1970s there began a number of tax revolts in various states and individual school districts aimed at reducing the mushrooming school budgets. The Arab oil embargo and the resulting inflation easily fanned the flames of the revolts for several years. And then there was "special education."

A federal law in 1975 mandated that schools use the "least restrictive" option when designing a child's educational program. This meant, if a child could be accommodated within the regular school building, it must be done. Many students with handicaps of various types suddenly were attending school. The expenses required to properly meet their needs were greater than when they were given minimal support outside of school.

School systems began to identify ("code") more and more regular students as having handicaps. Some teachers found the handicapping process a slick way to remove *difficult but normal* children from the classroom. Some anxious parents even succeeded in getting their essentially normal children coded so that their children would receive more personal attention. Already rising school budgets soared. The percentage of the budget dedicated only to the students with handicaps (real or not) grew to the detriment of regular education. This further incensed public opinion since there seemed no end to the remedial expenses and rising school budgets.

Educational damage caused by the medical model was not confined to school budgets and community-school relations. Many of the remedial services were conducted out of the classroom for various legitimate reasons. However, sometimes the students were removed so often each day or for such long periods that this proved to be disruptive to the flow of the class and weakened the important bond between the students serviced and the rest of the class.

In the desire to avoid charges of discrimination, public schools admitted students who had no business being in regular classrooms or even the school. Disruptions from the students' behavior or the modifications required in the class made life unreasonably difficult for the teachers and other students. The biggest price to be paid for the flawed medical model, however, surfaced only recently. It is the intrusion of the state and federal governments into the local schools.

In the past, state governments generally had been reluctant to use their lawful ability to interfere with local control of schools. The federal government was even less inclined to dictate. True, starting in the 1950s much federal money was offered to schools in an effort to improve reading, science and math. But even with this new infusion of money the percentage of local school costs paid by the federal government was quite small. Strings were few. Even forced integration was not aimed at the day-to-day tasks of the teachers. However, this hands-off approach was reversed in the '90s. While there was some genuine concern that schools were faltering, it became politically expedient for politicians at all levels to demand that society get tougher (once again!) on students and educators. If only they had known a little industrial history.

When an assembly line is pressured to exceed its limit, often the line will not respond because it simply cannot go faster or add more complexity. Lines that do try eventually show a decline in the quality of the product and/or the workers' health until the line breaks down altogether. There has been no magical elimination of student dropouts, absentees, vandalism, self-destructive behavior and general apathy with the latest educational reform. And demand for student remedial services (academic, medical and psychological) are at an all-time high.

The breakdown also is being seen among the workers. As mentioned earlier, many high-quality experienced teachers are no longer in the classroom. Their song is generally the same. They became fed up with years of constant teacher bashing and being told to do the impossible. Among those veterans still on the job are feelings of anger, frustration, resignation or apathy, qualities that undermine the quality of education. Although some public-service commercials and some high officials praise those who teach, this does not begin to fix the situation. As every single person with power or a selfish agenda demands that teachers do more, the teachers know that significant and permanent improvement is not possible with the present system.

As if problems from the native population are not enough, the largest wave of immigration in decades has further magnified the flaws of the system. Many new immigrants cannot speak English. Many have come from experiences of severe deprivation and violence. All come with their own culture. Schools do not have the flexible structure to smoothly and efficiently handle these many variations from the "norm." Adults looking for a job or job security need look no further than the area of remediation, including English-language services. The demand for help in these areas is unlimited.

It would be difficult to imagine an irony that is greater than the relationship among the medical model, today's educational reform effort and the actual results. The medical model was adopted years ago to fine tune the system. Instead, its use has played a significant part in creating more dissatisfaction and a demand for raising the bar. This demand is creating an even *greater* use of the medical model that in turn creates *even more* dissatisfaction with the educational system. As the educational wheel turns round and round, however, few see that the rat needs to jump off the wheel and do something different. Something far, far different.

∼

Scientific management stymies creativity and change in schools.

One January morning Christine showed up at my first-grade classroom door. This was the fifth school Christine had attended since September. This also was my introduction to the new "Okies," families that constantly were on the move, as during the Depression. At the moment, the other students were working on individual academic assignments so I was able to work with Christine alone and assess her abilities.

Christine's enrollment in midyear presented no problem to me or the other students. She simply would be "plugged" into the curriculums at the points best for her. If working in a particular group seemed appropriate for Christine, this would be done with a minimum of hassle since the groups frequently added and subtracted members. After my evaluations I assigned Valerie to be Christine's buddy and help her get started in the creative writing we did each morning. As Christine began to work I couldn't help but contrast her life with my own. During my seven years of elementary school I had remained in the same house and school the entire time.

∼

As usual, the door frame was covered with notes from the parents of my primary students indicating where each child was going after school. Every day was a different destination and rarely did a child go straight home. Today, many of the youngsters would go to T-Ball. Then came the announcement over the loudspeaker. Because of rain, T-Ball was canceled. The class erupted in loud cheers. The students knew they would be going home.

12

A World of Change
The Need for Flexibility

FROM TIME TO TIME a severely neglected or abused child makes news to underscore the relationship of environment to growth and learning. There have been many decades of private, local, state and federal government efforts to protect children and put them on an equal footing before and after school entrance. These efforts have been well-intentioned but ineffective. Here and there some children have had their condition improved at least temporarily. However, totally controlling the children's environment is not possible. There are many variables not within the control of government.

One obvious example is parents. Even with laws to guide behavior, the individual nature of parents makes for uneven compliance or interpretation. Another variable is the changing nature of governments. As officeholders change, there are philosophical differences and changes in child assistance. Consider the federal Head Start program.

Despite the inappropriate name (at best, the program can help children break even with more advantaged children), Head Start's key original goals made sense, especially the one to help parents become better caregivers. Eventually, however, increasing formal academic skills became a key goal. After years of controversy (and many studies) it was found that force feeding academic skills to preschoolers did not create significant and permanent improvement once the preschoolers were enrolled in elementary school. The emphasis then went back to the original goals.

Amazingly though, despite the overwhelming negative evidence, there still is serious talk of again increasing Head Start's formal academic content and, thereby, ignoring what young children really need first.

There are other variables that affect children's education that are double edged, ignored or even unrecognized by society. Medical science, perhaps surprisingly, is one such variable. On one hand it has increased the lifespan of children and made their daily life more pleasant. This, of course, makes for better students. On the other hand, medicine's advancements also have made more difficult the conducting of America's schools. For example, premature babies are being saved at earlier and earlier stages. As mentioned, however, the babies pay an educational price for being saved. Although the number of preemies and children saved from other health catastrophes still is a small percentage of students enrolled, these children place a strain on the rigid school structure far greater than their small numbers.

Another variable ignored or unrecognized is the change in the adult population. Many of today's adults do not want or are unable to accept the responsibilities of being adults. Until relatively recently, American society had come far since children were treated as miniature adults. Universal education laws rescued the children from the mine, mill and other dangerous adult jobs. Adults (and even teenagers) deliberately shielded the younger children from the racier or rougher aspects of society. Children were influenced primarily by the parents in the home, adult relatives, formal religious leaders and even neighbors. This has changed.

Science and technology are catalyzing tremendous changes throughout the world. These significant changes are occurring so rapidly that adults have a very difficult time adjusting to the changes. This strains or eliminates the anchors of society. In modern society the ability to define obvious right and wrong and to pass these values on to children has become impaired. Materialism, energized by good times following World War II, has intensified decade by decade at the expense of spirituality.

Adults throughout society have become obsessed with competition and the prizes for the winner, be they material or glory. Everything is for sale, it seems, be it an object or a reputation. Adults, harried by increasing time constraints, find it easier to make the quick, handy or tempting choice, without regard for the long-term costs. Into this moral chaos has come popular culture.

Modern popular culture, based on materialism, narcissism, the bizarre and the worship of youth has emerged as a major force in the upbringing of children. Technology has played a major role in the spread of this culture. Parents unwittingly have welcomed the new culture into the home by way of television, radio, computer and other electronic tools. Even outside the home the new culture is difficult to escape.

The electronic tools have become portable and ubiquitous, enabling the culture to surface in virtually every nook and cranny of American society, from grocery stores to the beach. Improved transportation and instant worldwide communications literally have spread pop culture to the far corners of the planet. The effect of this massive spread can be seen in the students' behavior, attitudes and learning in all schools. It is most obvious in public schools.

Some misbehavior in school always has been present, even in the strictest school. In the past, however, the behavior generally was of a temporary nature. The acts were usually corrected in school or with a note to the parents. Extreme and violent behavior (apart from fist fights among the boys) was infrequent.

Today, misbehavior is more frequent, coarser and present even in very young children. For example, it is not unknown today for five and six year olds to use the obscene language not learned and used in the past until the teenage years. It also is not unusual for the same young children to talk freely about serious adult subjects such as sexual intercourse, abortion, murder and the use of drugs. On occasion, some of the young children act out these adult subjects right in the classroom. Historically, most violators of rules in school were boys and this still is true. However, misbehavior by girls is increasing, including many of the more serious violations.

The extent of the negative change in children's behavior might be epitomized by two everyday examples and one that is rare. The first is the simple task of lining up or sitting in a group. Many of today's elementary children have a compulsion to touch, poke, push and otherwise disturb someone if they are near. They have little conception of personal space and privacy.

The second example is traveling to and from school on a school bus. At the very least, the noise level of the students reflects a lack of self-control. Of more concern, obnoxious, unsafe and aggressive (even violent) behavior has become so prevalent that concerned parents do not allow their children to ride the school bus. The use of bus monitors and cameras might seem to indicate a resolve by school personnel to maintain order. In reality, such measures more strongly indicate the failure of adults to socialize the children as they are growing up.

The homicidal violence committed by students on teachers and entire student populations also must be mentioned. Considering the number of students in all schools, the attackers have been few. However, the level of violence in several ferocious attacks of recent years was unheard of in past generations.

The most disturbing part of the change in children's behavior (and perhaps it is indicative) is the reaction of parents. Instead of shouldering the responsibility for their children's misbehavior, a significant percentage of parents deny that there is a problem and become defensive or even belligerent towards the school staff or other authorities. Other parents might show concern but lack the common sense or will to correct their children. Their sense of helplessness highlights both a lack of moral steel in many parents and the power of the new culture that spawns the lesser values. This surrendering of parental influence and duty is reflected daily in schools, as considerable time must be spent on law and order before dealing with the curriculum.

Some parents with well-behaved children respond with the best of intentions but make long-range mistakes. To protect their children, these parents run from the values/discipline problem by quitting the school. Freedom of choice is good to have. However, enrolling children in private schools or home schooling just to hide from a problem is only a short-run solution. Unresolved student difficulties in public or private schools eventually affect our entire society as troubled "Little Billy" grows up and travels about with his problems.

Schools have changed somewhat to deal with this destructive flux in society. The guidance counselor, once not found until the seventh grade, now has become an essential part of the elementary school and already is overburdened. The counselor (and teachers) not only deal with student problems but, more and more, deal with *parental* problems that used to be handled by religious leaders, adult relatives and family friends.

Local police now patrol the hallways of some schools and in others try to teach what parents should have taught at home (for example, the DARE program). But such measures only address the symptoms of the students' problems and do not change the schools' inflexibility. Even in the world of yesterday, there were enough variables to discredit a rigid approach to education. Today's world cries out desperately for a school structure that has maximum flexibility.

∼

Society's new problems require maximum school flexibility.

As the camera panned the "gifted and talented" sixth graders dissecting owl pellets, the TV reporter gushed about the school's gifted and talented program. As I watched the television, I had mixed emotions. All of my six- and seven-year-old students did tasks of this nature every day, including the owl pellets.

∼

Roger was a highly sociable, intelligent and artsy six year old. From the beginning, his discussions and creative writing were unusual and disturbing, sometimes with bizarre sexual themes. When the art teacher felt compelled to warn me of his unsettling art work I was not surprised. Roger was living in a world of fantasy more typical of a troubled adult. When I broached my concern with the college-educated parents I was rebuffed. At least part of this denial, I suspected, was related to the parents' loose lifestyle, which included partying with drugs.

13

The Decline of Rome
The Collapse of the Better Students

UNLIKE THE REFORM MOVEMENT caused by the launching of the satellite Sputnik, the current reform movement is a result of an accumulation of events. As western Europe and Japan modernized in the decades following World War II, the advantage of American business and industry slowly began to shrink. Major American companies such as the auto makers greatly accelerated this change by not raising their standards to match foreign competition. American products and thinking eventually developed a reputation, partly deserved, as being second rate. The resulting loss of business shocked the American business world. This stimulated the reemphasis of quality, initiative and creativity and, when combined with recession overseas, eventually led to a partial rejuvenation. However, the quest for profits above all had generated some irreversible momentum. Manufacturing jobs began to disappear overseas.

Unfairly, American education was linked to the turmoil in the workplace. Students, it was said, were not learning enough or were not learning the right skills to compete worldwide. As in the past, the most visible of these critics did not come from the classroom but from business, industry and politics. And as usual, the criticism was leveled primarily at the classroom teacher.

Some educational leaders responded to the criticism with a variation of the old panacea of pressure called "minimum competencies." Each student was supposed to master at least a particular set of skills by the end of a specific period (such as grades three, eight and twelve). This was the forerunner of today's state and federally mandated tests but often constructed and administered at a local level. Like No Child Left Behind, the minimum competencies broke no new ground.

Another response was the selection of students for "gifted and talented" programs. Gifted and talented programs affected relatively few students and from the beginning there was (and still is today) no consensus among the nation's many school districts as to the meaning of gifted and talented, what should be included in the curriculum and how it should be taught. As schools wasted time, money and goodwill on these two ineffective responses, these efforts masked for a time the key catalyst to the present reform movement: the decline of the children of the "elite."

There is considerable disagreement about the academic performance of middle- and upper-class students in the last three decades. Some insist that achievement has been declining while others insist scores have been stable or even inching upwards. The fact that there is a debate at all says a lot (Why don't we know the answer?). If performance *is* down, the adults certainly have helped. Consider higher education.

In recent decades colleges have greatly expanded enrollments. To do this, many students have been accepted who would not be considered prepared, some even to the point of being functionally illiterate. In the past, the rigor of college usually weeded out those few students who did not belong. However, of late this has not been the case as grade inflation, "gut" courses and less than rigorous majors have come into more general use. The beginning of this decline in collegiate standards mirrored a similar decline at the high school level.

At some point there began a weakening in the number and type of core courses required to graduate from high school (for example, foreign language not required, fewer years of math). Grade inflation appeared at this level, also, increasing the honor rolls. Free time during the school day became more prevalent and some students were able to finish the required curriculum long before the end of the senior year. With the present emphasis on state- and federal-mandated standards and the use for several years of advanced placement courses (the quality of which is subject to much debate), it might be assumed that high school has reversed itself and is becoming at least as rigorous as before. This remains to be seen.

A related topic of discussion that surfaces from time to time is the fatigue of high school students. It is argued that they cannot be alert early in the morning and that their life is so busy that they do not get enough sleep. Various reasons have been put forth, such as too much homework, too many after-school activities, too many hours working in retail jobs and the biological nature of teenagers. Other reasons suggested are the long trips to and from school and the stress of having parents with separate households (different sets of rules, for example). The troubling aspect of this particular debate is the lack of common sense shown by the adults.

If a high school student must work to help keep the family afloat, the student should take fewer courses per year and extend the time to graduation. Working in all other cases needs to take a back seat to studying. The teachers should work in concert to assign reasonable amounts of homework. Extra-curricular activities (including sports) and activities independent of the school must be done so that they do not disrupt education and the family routine. Students need to get to bed at a reasonable hour.

Most crucial of all, parents must make a better effort to stabilize (that is, slow down and simplify) their own lives and nurture their marriages. Such all-too-obvious solutions make more sense than officially inflating all SAT scores and assuming teenagers are biologically unable to stay awake before 8:00 a.m.

The debate over academic deterioration in the older elite students has caught the public's attention because our society historically has focused on the end product of the assembly line. Unfortunately, the deterioration extends to the youngest students also. This deterioration is not easy to see using regular benchmarks. Although it is true that many school districts have used commercial standardized tests for years, the testing has not necessarily been done on a regular basis at the elementary level and the results used in an efficient and consistent way.

It also must be remembered that the youngest students are emerging scholars and each student is so individual, as is each school and town. Together, all these factors make it difficult if not impossible to compare elementary students academically over past years. On the other hand, at all grade levels a decline in the physical, social and emotional areas over the years is more easy to see. It is logical, therefore, to conclude that decline in these three areas has led to an academic decline, also.

Much discussion has been generated in recent years about modern students' inability to sit still and focus on a task or speaker. Although some argue for poor discipline at home as a cause (making the behavior, in theory, correctable), others argue that the poor behavior is a permanent physical change caused by environmental factors. Unfortunately, other negative changes also have come to light. As the students become more and more sedentary, both in and out of school, the number of obese students is increasing. Asthma and diabetes, once uncommon among the young, are becoming more common. It is ironic that as science and technology have increasingly protected students from past stresses such as famine, contagious disease and poverty, the improvements have spawned new threats to the students' physical condition. These new threats when combined with the less explainable "hyperactivity" create significant obstacles to learning.

When studying the social and emotional status of a child, it is difficult to separate the two areas. Loosely defined, the social has to deal with how a child reacts in particular situations with other people. The emotional overlaps the social. It deals with a child's self-image and how the child reacts to life's situations, social or not. Students who are socially and emotionally stable naturally are far more likely to succeed in school than students who are not.

A long-standing assumption is that social and emotional

stability corresponds to wealth. Children of the rich and middle class are assumed to be "civilized" and, thus, models for those less fortunate. At the same time, the poorer students are expected to bring considerable social and emotional baggage from home. There is some truth in this stereotype since poverty limits opportunity and creates stress. Conveniently overlooked, however, are the poor that become model school citizens and leaders. These successes are due to factors even stronger than money: high moral values and discipline instilled by the parents. Also overlooked is the fact that students of better means can and do burden society. This point has been driven home in recent years by the social and emotional collapse of the elite students.

The seeds of the collapse were planted many years ago as the country industrialized, the population started to concentrate and life's pace increased. Eventually, in the roughest of the big city high schools knives began to replace fists. Crudely made handguns then replaced knives. In hindsight, this escalation of weapons was ominous. Yet, even one generation ago deaths were rare. Today, the violence is startling from any perspective.

It is occurring at all school levels and in geographical areas once thought not prone to violence. The weapons being used are often sophisticated. The violence is being committed not only against those who are considered enemies but also deliberately against the most innocent of bystanders. The shootings are premeditated and not sparked by sudden rage, self-defense or even necessarily by bad grades. Of particular concern is that the violent students show no concern for their own future and no remorse. And they are white and not poor.

These very violent students are few but are the tip of an iceberg of social and emotional problems. Self-destructive behavior such as cheating, suicide (and thinking about doing it), the use of drugs and alcohol and improper sexual behavior not only is at epidemic levels among teenagers but has spread as low as the elementary-aged children. The elite children are just as likely, sometimes more likely, to be involved in this destructive behavior as anyone else. None of this should be a surprise. The children are responding to the world their elders have made for them.

It is difficult to exaggerate the extent of the negative psychological situation of today's children. Consider some indirect evidence. Many decades ago psychiatrists and psychologists began to use children's art to screen for and diagnose psychological problems. The Gesell Institute began to use art for a different purpose, to measure the normal social and emotional growth of young children. In particular, the Institute used children's drawings of people. For reasons unknown, up to about the age of nine or ten a child inadvertently reveals his social and emotional age when making a person. Dr. Frances Ilg of the Institute later determined that tree drawings also could be used for the same purpose.

Experienced developmental examiners soon learned to spot indications of psychological abnormality if they appeared in the children's person and tree drawings. Such discoveries, of course, were not the intention of the developmental evaluation and the examiners (usually teachers) were not qualified to diagnose and treat psychological problems. Students who showed red flags, however, at least could be referred for further investigation and possible treatment by qualified adults.

Since 1976 I have done thousands of developmental evaluations of students from ages four and a half to nine in various communities of various states. The change in the art work over the years is frightening. Fewer and fewer young children show social and emotional stability in their art work. More and more show symptoms of psychological problems. What is being revealed on paper unfortunately matches the behavior seen today both in and out of school. The negative changes are occurring wholesale in children of all types, *including the children of the elite.*

Trying to read the children's social and emotional developmental levels today is more difficult, as more negative psychological clues intermingle with the developmental. Certainly, though, the children's art work suggests strongly that they are less mature for their grade placement than in the past.

It took a while but power brokers in business, industry and government eventually realized that inferior academic performance, however measured, was no longer confined to the lower class. Their cries of outrage have been widely credited with starting the current educational reform movement. However, in essence it was the social/emotional slide of the elite children that was the catalyst.

∽

Psychological problems among schoolchildren are increasing across the board.

For many years New Hampshire supported the educational independence of every school district. However, this meant that most funds to support a district came from local sources and not the state. Eventually, some of the poorer districts sued the state for nonsupport.

In 1993 the state supreme court ruled that the state must guarantee the funding of an adequate education for all students.

In 1997 the state supreme court ruled that the state's lukewarm response to the original decision was unconstitutional.

In 2006 a state superior court judge ruled that the state's most recent funding plan still was unconstitutional.

As the wealthier New Hampshire cities and towns continue to fight with all legal and political means not to share funds with poorer districts, the state finds itself not alone. According to the Education Commission of the States, forty-four of fifty states have been sued or are being sued over educational funding.

∼

One of my first-grade mothers stopped by my room after school. "You know," she said with a wry smile, "even though Len is now doing well in school, I never believed that stuff Mrs. Kellogg (the kindergarten teacher), Mrs. Allen (the pre-first-grade teacher) and you said about my child's development. Until now, that is." I looked at the mother, who had only grudgingly accepted the school's advice about extra time and asked what had caused the change. "I took Len to the dentist yesterday," she said. "Len's almost seven and a half now but the dentist looked at his x-rays and said 'Your son has a nice six-year-old mouth.' "

14

The Simplicity of the Problem
The Quagmire of Denial and Ignorance

THE PRESENT SCHOOL REFORM movement is the most complex of the many historical attempts to reform education. It involves the federal and state governments. Even the colleges and universities, despite their past aloofness, have been dragged into it. The media attention is immense. Even considering the effect of inflation, the money being spent dwarfs any funds spent in the past. Yet results so far have been *minimal*. The attempt to raise achievement levels even to those of the past have yielded, dollar for dollar and hour for hour of effort, very little. As mentioned, the reform movement resembles in its most important parts the failed movements of the past. It is a shame to waste the country's resources when true reform is possible. Thinking must radically change.

One crucial change would be for the public to acknowledge that there are serious problems that involve *every* student and that *major* change is needed. Contrary to popular belief, this consensus has not occurred. Getting there will be a challenge considering that humans tend to be parochial and creatures of habit.

People like and need routine to bring order to their lives. Once set in a routine, however, many people resist change—even if the routine is uncomfortable or detrimental and, illogically, sometimes even when the change is known to be beneficial. In education this inertia is supported by the influence of the bell curve and excessive faith in and obedience to authority. This creates a mind set that makes it easy to deny the need for change.

There also is a tendency for people to focus first on their own lives. This means that their primary interest in education is local. As long as their school system or, in the case of parents, their own children seem to be doing well, adults believe there is no need for change. It is always the "other" school or system that needs fixing. Yet when it is time for resources to be divided, adults want their own system or school to have top priority. This inability or refusal to see the big picture makes any attempt at reform difficult and painfully slow.

Of course, there always have been some who have recognized the extent of the problem (if not the remedy) and have fled rather than fight or have fought and lost. Perhaps the percentage of these people is greater today. If so, this has not helped in bringing a consensus since the majority still thinks small picture.

Ironically, the success of having so many citizens in the educational system works against a consensus on what must be done. Not only do most citizens have an opinion on education, many consider themselves experts based solely on their experience as students. However, the forced nature of this experience makes them emotionally involved and not necessarily objective in their thinking. Their experience of many years ago is limited in scope. It is true that former (and ongoing) students can accurately identify and articulate obvious problems such as boring teachers, classes that are too large and leaky roofs. Many of the biggest problems, however, are complex, subtle and hidden from the view of students and taxpayers.

Getting additional education and work beyond high school might seem likely to give adults a broader and better educational perspective. Leaders in business and industry, for example, can judge the effectiveness of the general educational system in the performance of their workers. Yet, the number of schools and systems, geographical regions, different local histories and ethnic and religious factions is vast. Determining what is needed for a single school or system is challenging enough, much less determining common national needs.

Considering these obstacles and the failure of past efforts, true educational reform may seem impossible. However, the experience of developmental reformers showed that adults have a willingness, even an eagerness, to make major educational change if they are provided sufficient information. Specifically, this means that everyone, the public and educators alike, needs to know how we got to where we are now in education.

Much of this vital information is unlikely to come from the educational profession. Most current educators know little more of the big picture than the public. In theory, educators should know the past. Regardless of the institution attended, prospective teachers usually take a number of similar courses. One of these is the "history of education." Unfortunately, this course tends to be general in scope and starts far back in world history. The experience of the ancient educators is interesting but is not put into a context that is useful in modern society.

Even more up-to-date information specific about our country provides little of the needed nitty-gritty to the beginning teacher or future superintendent. Educators begin their career thinking that what they see being done for children and are told to do is tried, true and sacred. Little do they know that much of what is done is due to politics and economics—not the children's needs—and this has been the unwritten rule from the beginning.

Assuming that the majority recognizes that major change is needed, what next? Which practices should be discarded or avoided? Which ones are good and should be retained or added? The answer is absurdly simple. Use the knowledge of child development to make all decisions. The basic theories of the major theorists in the last hundred years have been validated by past classroom experience, both good and bad. Do not waste this proven knowledge.

Assume every child is normal and an educational sponge until proven otherwise. This means that when a child learns immediately, the skill chosen to be studied and the practice being used is correct. On the other hand, incorrect adult choices are revealed by inefficiency, excessive struggle and failure. In general, learning is a natural and interesting activity. When a task is avoided regardless of enticement, something is wrong but probably not with the student. These principles are true regardless of gender, religion, economic or ethnic background. Doubters will be tempted to state that there is never a simple solution to a complex problem. Yet, every classroom or school that has taken even the smallest step in individualizing its program has shown immediate and dramatic student improvement.

The following chapters are not an encyclopedia of how to teach this and that. There are already many good books that provide very specific teaching ideas in most subject areas. Rather, the chapters use many of the typical school subjects as examples of how child development and the resource of time and timing are crucial to virtually all aspects of education. Many people intimately familiar with schools no doubt will remember particular schools using the discussed practices to some degree. This is the frustration and shame of the situation. Not only has the need for change been obvious for decades but in bits and pieces true reform has been floating all around us, unrecognized by most.

∽

Denial and ignorance prevent true reform.

PART II

THE COMMON THREAD OF TIME

Rachel's mom was a volunteer in her child's primary classroom. She had just finished helping Billy do a math activity, so we were able to take a few seconds to talk.

"How do you do it?" she asked. "They're all so different! Billy can count to ten but still needs his fingers. And then there's Lance. Yesterday he counted past a hundred by two's. He also knows his coins."

I smiled and nodded. The parents of the twenty-four students were a mixed bag. Their occupations included plumber, engineer, housewife, clerk, truck driver, logger and medical doctor, among others. Many of the kids had two parents but one's mother was a widow and four had "absent" fathers. It was logical that the children were also a mixed bag.

~

I was subbing in a fifth-grade class where I spotted some revealing data on the front board. When a student didn't get his or her classroom work done during the day, the regular teacher put the child's name on the board with the unfinished assignment. The board was filling up with names and, believe it or not, it looked like this:

Liza Math: pages 21, 22, 23, 24–26, 29, 34, 35, 36, 38, 39–40, 43
      Reading: pages 215–245, 247–267, 269–301, 303, 305, 307

Brad Spelling: pages 7, 8, 10–12, 14, 15, 16, 18, 21, 22, 25–27, 28
      Math: pages 20, 24, 25, 26, 30–32, 34, 35, 40–41, 43, 44, 46
      Social studies: pages 215, 216, 220–224, 226–230, 231

I was stunned. Didn't anyone—teacher, principal, guidance counselor—realize what was happening?

15

First Impressions
Evaluating a School

> "...there must be no gulf between the home and school."
>
> — Johann Pestalozzi
> Swiss Educator and Reformer
> (1746–1827)

EACH SCHOOL MUST BE evaluated separately. There are good, bad and indifferent public *and* private schools at all levels. In a bad system a fair or even good school can exist. In a highly regarded system there can be a so-so or poor school. The first indication of a school's worth is how a child and school first meet.

Most schools have the same standard procedure for the young first-time student. The parent brings the child to school for registration. This involves paperwork to prove the child is eligible, medical screening and, in many schools, some sort of testing. This first contact between school and family is almost too late. Schools should not be seen as an abrupt change in a child's and family's life but as a natural and welcome extension of home. To accomplish this the school should have an outreach program.

An outreach program provides helpful information to adults who are prospective parents or have children too young for school. For example, the school should regularly mail to these adults information on child raising and health care. Also part of the mailing should be school newsletters and invitations to school functions that are open to the public. Long before registration the child and *both* parents should have visited the school many times.

Another clue to the school's quality is its openness. In the past, schools were similar to a castle with its drawbridge up. Visitors during school time were greatly discouraged. To a large extent, this unfriendly attitude has been reversed. Volunteers in the classroom (especially at the elementary level), libraries and at special school events are symbolic of this openness.

A good school even goes so far as to remove obstacles for parents wanting to help out. If, say, an elementary student has a baby sibling, the student's parent is allowed to bring the young one into the classroom while volunteering. Stiff-necked adults might be horrified by such an idea but the best schools at all levels nurture teaching techniques and classroom systems that are flexible and thrive on unique situations.

There is no better way for any adult to learn about a school than to become part of it. A perceptive citizen who frequently volunteers usually develops greater educational insight such as how *different* each child is. In turn, these differences make clear to this same volunteer the near impossibility of meeting the many different needs based on rigid timelines and arbitrary curricular expectations. Even when helping a teacher who heroically bucks the rigid system, however, the volunteer still might spot vestiges of the castle mentality. One such vestige is the classroom door.

There are many teachers who feel insecure unless the classroom door is shut. This defensive behavior is caused by various factors. The teachers might not trust their superiors or the evaluation system. They may not be confident in themselves or, despite great self-confidence, they may realize they are fighting an unfair and risky battle. Consider evaluations alone.

In the past, despite formal evaluation procedures, impressions were formed by the principal when walking by a classroom door. Such "walk-by" evaluations were dreaded by teachers since great weight was given to the teachers' ability to keep students quiet and still. Yet, from time to time all students get talkative, restless, difficult to handle or (a great irony) excited by school work. Also, sometimes even a master teacher has a bad moment or day.

Thus, the chances of an unfavorable walk-by evaluation are all too good if the door is open. Although there have been some attempts to improve the evaluation process, the improvements have been threatened by recent attempts to link evaluations to test scores. Thus, the process is still unsatisfactory.

Interacting with superficial evaluations is the teachers' own education. For many years new teachers left college thinking that they should or had to work alone. Admitting that they needed help and did not know all the answers was not always seen as an option. Some teacher-preparation courses have begun to emphasize the need for openness with the public and collaboration with colleagues. Some schools are using staff mentors, sometimes right in the classroom, to help new teachers. These are good first steps because closed doors—real or psychological—convey a "keep out" message to everyone, even other teachers. Some teachers put a "Please come in!" sign on their closed doors but this does not fully overcome an initial negative impression.

Openness may be a sign of a good school also because the best teaching practices, learning and the zeal for more learning are catalyzed by a free-flowing atmosphere that is school wide. This atmosphere should be found in all usable spaces in the school, including the hallways, cafeteria and grounds, not just the official classrooms. Free-flowing schools radiate human energy and a sense of purpose. Perceptive visitors can quickly get a sense of this positive flow—or lack of it.

Despite concerns about security, it is vital that the progress made in the interaction among school, community and family be continued. Not only is this an important way for the community and parents to evaluate each school, it is also an important way for schools to foster support for treating each child as an individual.

∼

**A frequent school visitor is impressed by
the individual nature of each child.**

I was finding it difficult to implement the new health curriculum adopted a year earlier by the district curriculum committee. Its vast scope would do justice to a premedical college program and with the beefed up language arts, math and science curriculums there just wasn't time in the day. Then the school board dropped a bomb. It mandated that we add a K-6 citizenship curriculum to all the others.

∼

Ben was eight when he transferred into my third/fourth-grade combination class from a school in upstate New York. His report card falsely indicated he was up to "grade level" in reading. In fact, he was barely more than a beginning reader and, not surprisingly, he lacked overall confidence and was not happy to be in school.

The solution was simple and obvious but would take several months. I started Ben in a reading program of very short stories that gradually increased in difficulty. He was successful from the start and, as his skills improved, so did his attitude towards school. The reading program did not make Ben self-conscious because each student was successful at his or her level. Of course, everyone knew what the reading pecking order was in class but the students did not officially compete against each other and the best readers were not treated as royalty.

16

The Meat of the Subject
Molding the Curriculums to the Child

> *"A gardener takes more pains with the young than with the full grown plant and men commonly find it needful in any undertaking to begin well."*
> — Francis Bacon
> English Philosopher
> (1561–1626)

IN MOST SCHOOL SYSTEMS the curriculums are in a constant state of change. This is a normal and healthy process. While it is often debated what should be taught in any curriculum or whether new curriculums need to be added, there is usually more agreement than not.

School systems long ago developed a common academic core that included such subjects as math, reading, writing and history. This core has received constant and strong emphasis over the years while other subjects such as science, music, art and health have received inconsistent and/or weaker support. Also agreed upon long ago was that each subject should be taught in a sequential fashion, building complex skills from layers of easier skills. This general agreement on the nature of curriculum was true whether in an urban, suburban or country school and in every state. Yet, with the recent emphasis on raising the bar, the public might think that curriculums had been neglected over the years. This is an ironic concern.

In the last few decades the biggest problem with curriculums has been that there are *too many* of them and the ones in place are *too extensive.* This came about because educational leaders under pressure are often eager to add to the teachers' plate. Unfortunately, nothing is ever taken away. If there ever was a time when teachers were able to thoroughly cover their assigned material in the time given, this certainly is not true today.

Even if curriculums are properly constructed, however, this is not enough to foster learning. There must be a proper delivery system. Whether parents enroll their first child in kindergarten or an older child in a new school, they are anxious for a smooth transition. They console themselves in part with an assumption that the schools are well organized to deliver the curriculums. This is a false assumption.

Years ago, if new students could show proof of age, residency and a shot card they were immediately placed "cold" in a classroom (sometimes in the middle of the day and a lesson) solely based on their age. Few schools made the attempt to find out if the new students' classroom experience and expertise were similar to that of their new classmates before starting the new students. Fewer schools made the attempt to determine if the new students had the developmental maturity to meet the demands of the class.

If the new students could not speak English this compounded their lack of skills and maturity exponentially. Even the sharpest of immigrants found this situation almost unbearable. It is a popular myth (fostered by the idea of "rugged individualism") that most immigrants in the past rose above classroom obstacles and thrived. In truth, many dropped out. Today the situation is not much different for new students, native born or immigrant.

Outwardly, there are differences. The youngest children enrolling for the first time are screened for physical and intellectual problems. However, because of the bell curve and medical model, the intent is to determine which students are deficient and need a cure. Unless there is a huge and very glaring deficit, the children are still placed cold according to their birth certificate. Students who transfer from other schools are placed according to the grade they were in last. Records are then requested by mail from the previous school. This procedure takes several days and sometimes weeks. The sharpest teachers sometimes call the previous school for quicker (and unofficial) information but this often cannot be done until after the child actually enters the classroom.

Non-English-speaking immigrants are provided with some kind of interpretive assistance (*if* it is available and the school has the funds) and English instruction. How to instruct non-English speakers is controversial but the intent is still to place them on the educational assembly line as quickly as possible. And the children's ages and the limited time of the school structure are there to shape and force the most well-intentioned efforts.

With a flexible school structure, the situation for new students is reversed. No child walks into school cold and starts the same day. Everything possible is learned about a student so that the curriculum and classroom will fit the child from the first. Only then does the child enter a classroom. The following scenario is an example of how a flexible school structure uses time and timing to ensure a proper entrance and use of the curriculums.

∼

It is 9:00 a.m. on October 15. Susie Smith's family has just moved into town. Susie has never been to school before but now she is eligible in her new town. The school district has a requirement to be age five by October 1. Susie's fifth birthday was September 27. When Susie and her parents arrive at the new school, the students have been in session for almost six weeks. After a welcome by the principal, a tour of the school by a sixth grader is given (a prestigious chore for the older students). Then the parents sit down for a talk with the principal.

She gives them an overview of how the school operates and asks some general information questions about and of Susie. Then the principal gives the parents several documents, to be completed later, including a health history form. It is vital that the school knows if Susie has had a difficult birth or any serious illnesses, injuries or experiences. The parents have left Susie's shot card at home. This is O.K. No student is allowed to start the same day anyway. The Smiths are asked to come back at the end of the school day. All documents, including the card, should be dropped off then.

At 3:00 the family returns. Susie meets with a number of staff members. The nurse provides a medical screening, including a vision and hearing check. A primary-grade teacher gives a developmental test to Susie, one that the parents are encouraged to watch. The test measures Susie's growth intellectually, physically, socially and emotionally. If the registration paperwork or screening tests raise questions about Susie's status, further testing will be done the next day. The results of the testing are discussed with the parents but not in the presence of Susie.

Mrs. Green is introduced to the parents. She teaches a "primary" classroom and will be Susie's teacher for the next two to four years. The parents react with surprise. Isn't Susie going to kindergarten? Yes and no responds the principal. She gives a copy of the curriculum to the parents. The document is a sequential list of skills in all the academic areas for children ages four to nine. All classes in the school are of mixed chronological ages, explains the principal, much like a family. Every day, all the students work together at times, but Susie also will be given an individualized program to meet her specific needs.

The parents seem confused. What determines how long Susie stays with Mrs. Green they ask? The principal defers to Mrs. Green. The teacher explains that she will meet frequently with the Smiths. As long as they all agree that Susie's needs are being met, Susie will stay with Mrs. Green.

The Smiths thumb through the curriculum. It is detailed and seems comprehensive. But why are the skills as low as age four and as high as nine? The teacher again does the talking. Each child is an individual and comes to school with a different background, potential for learning and level of growth. Each class must be flexible. The principal explains that the "middle elementary" and "upper elementary" classes continue the sequence of skills that the

Smiths have in their hands, with an equally wide spread at both ends. If a child needs more time to grow and learn, she states, then the time is provided. If a child can and *should* handle more advanced work in a subject, the curriculum and classroom structure allow this, also.

Mr. Smith, sort of a "Type A" personality, perks up over this flexibility. He asks if it will be possible for Susie to skip a grade if she can do the advanced portion of the curriculum. She already is beginning to read on her own. The eyes of the principal and Mrs. Green briefly meet. Mrs. Green explains that children need time to grow in all areas and this cannot be rushed without harming the child. The principal chips in by pointing to the curriculum and emphasizing how comprehensive it is. Each child is challenged on an individual basis, she states. However, to excel academically and to develop equally important social skills, a child must have social and emotional peers in the classroom. Besides, she adds, we have no first grade, second grade, and so forth, here. Nobody fails a grade or is promoted. The approach is called "continuous progress education." Susie may start tomorrow and will be placed in math, reading, and so on, according to the spots in the curriculum that are best for her. She will stay at the school until the parents and school staff agree she is ready to move on.

On the way home Mrs. Smith is outwardly ecstatic. She has seen how different each of her three young children are, how they each have progressed at different rates in learning to walk, talk and all other skills. How wonderful to have a school for Susie that is prepared for the differences among children! Mr. Smith is quiet. Mrs. Smith notes this silence, knows what it means and knows they will have to talk later. He'll come around, she thinks with confidence, when Susie succeeds day after day after day.

∽

The curriculums should be molded to each student.

"Can I stay in and finish my story?"

The primary class had just been told to line up for recess. I looked at Mae and shook my head. "No. You'll have time later. Besides, there's always tomorrow," I said.

As the students settled down in line I gave them the once over. Mae and two friends had lined up with paper and pencils. I tried to act stern.

"Put your papers and pencils back on your desks. This is recess."

"Aw," they groaned in unison. "We want to do more work."

"Go run around," I said. "Get some exercise. Play some games."

Mae made one last unsuccessful pitch. "Can we take out some books? We want to play school."

∽

Jimmy was being punished (again) with an in-school suspension and I was assigned to supervise him all day. The tiny workroom had no distractions such as windows and wall displays and I sat within reach. By the end of the day, however, I was impressed by how little work Jimmy had accomplished. He was a master of excuses as to why he couldn't start or finish. Even when he looked busy, close scrutiny revealed nothing happening.

17

The Big Mo
Success Breeds Success

YEARS AGO SOME SAGE coined the phrase "rat race" to refer to the darker side of science, technology and the resulting pace of modern life. In a world changing so quickly because of new knowledge and tools, humans tend to feel pressured by an irresistible flow of events. A constant fear of falling behind is pervasive, with little or no hope of improving the situation. In many ways American education in the last hundred years has reflected the increasing intensity of society's rat race.

The parents of hypothetical Susie Smith were not overly concerned that the school year had already begun. They still believed in the historical goal of kindergarten as an introduction to school. However, if Susie had been transferring into a higher grade, the parents' conversation with the school staff would have reflected great tension. Susie's late entrance would have meant that she was "behind" and had to "catch up" or fail the grade.

Kindergarten, a German word for "children's garden," is supposed to be a place for children to gradually and gently begin their schooling. Unfortunately, this original purpose is being eroded. The tension caused by the competitiveness of modern life and year after year of school bashing has resulted in academic and behavioral demands being pushed down in the grades, even as far as private preschool.

Anxious parents look for preschools (and private kindergartens) that will give their children an edge when they get into the "real" grades. Feeling the pressure and wanting to stay in business, many preschools are all too eager to oblige. They advertise that they teach reading. Their names often show this academic intensity. A few of these schools even rank the students academically!

Educational "experts" (who never seem to be practicing teachers) add fuel to the fire: all children after age one should go to daycare with "learning curriculums." All four year olds can and should be taught to read. Head Start should have a rigorous academic emphasis.

The anxiety of the parents is further increased by a heightened sense of danger. Instant communications, instant access to information and rapid transportation have made many people almost obsessed with life's dangers—real, low threat and even hypothetical. Education is seen more and more as one important way (some say the only way) to shield children from these dangers. Thus, school curriculums have been added for health, drugs and alcohol, driving and just about anything else that might be risky. Even financial curriculums to protect against consumer, investor and business dangers have been advocated. The problem with this defensive thinking is that biology has been forgotten.

It is true that all mammal young *are* vulnerable. However, there are developmental limits as to what lessons of life can be absorbed efficiently at a particular age. It is the job of the adults to protect the young as life's lessons are learned gradually and in a logical manner. One of the best ways for adults to provide protection in today's world is not to force children into the rat race but to quit it. Quitting the rat race does not mean ignoring life. Rather, it means to recognize the forces of modern society that are affecting us adversely and to modify them. For example, one of the best ways to slow down and simplify life is to avoid popular culture at home.

Using the TV, computer, computer games, CD player and phone minimally, selectively or not at all accomplishes many things. It encourages people to talk to each other face to face, to find creative things to do, keeps the noise down (thereby enlarging the house or apartment) and helps prevent dilution of parental values. Having such a sanctuary has a tremendous impact upon family members. Parents are more likely to recognize the natural rhythms of life and the natural progression of learning. This makes them more patient with their children and less anxious about their children's future. When the children come to school they reflect this lack of pressure and anxiety.

Families in which adults have quit the rat race also manage their time more wisely outside of the home. Although the children do participate in outside activities, the emphasis is such that the family remains in balance. Whether money is tight or plentiful, the parents maintain work schedules that are also in balance. Again, the children reflect positively their parents' values in the classroom. This may sound too good to be true in today's world, but I have had experience with students from such households. As a group, these children are more creative, eager to learn, disciplined, unselfish and well behaved than the other students.

The more a school is developmentally oriented and emphasizes individual continuous progress, the less it is part of the rat race. The more patient the school is with skill introduction and teaching, the better the children learn. When a child is introduced to a skill at the right time, success is immediate. The child then wants to study *more*.

As success piles upon success, the child is stimulated to take the initiative for learning. Independent learning eventually becomes the most important part of the child's waking day. Failure is shrugged off as merely a temporary setback. This "educational momentum" can be seen in schools today among those students who fit the assembly line accidentally or (because of developmental placement) by design.

At the elementary level there are students who try to take books and pencils out to recess so that they can continue their class work or start an independent task. They bring projects and artifacts from home so they can share their learning with others. Their enthusiasm for learning is contagious and spreads even among those students who are less dedicated. In the past this love for learning was attributed to the fact that these students were born "smart" or came from "good" families. The reality is that accidentally meshing with the curriculum had a lot to do with their educational momentum.

The success of proper timing and use of time (accidental or not) should not be a surprise for educators because there are many recorded examples of this. Students from well-adjusted families, who were kept out of school or were not able to enroll (such as missionary children) and then entered two or three years late, had no trouble once enrolled. They found the initial parts of the curriculum easy and quickly reached the level thought appropriate for their peers. In many cases they continued to soar *beyond*.

Other examples of educational momentum abound in reading instruction. Normal students who were introduced to formal reading later than usual quickly reached the level of those who were instructed because of their grade placement. Then, as a rule, the late starters went *beyond* their peers.

Advocates for early schooling and remedial services frown at the idea of later enrollment. They point to students who come from dysfunctional families or who have other legitimate obstacles to learning even before school entrance. It is true that the sooner problems are addressed, the better. The family, however, plays an indispensable role in the upbringing of children. No government agency can be the substitute. If the family is not ideal, it is best if the family is strengthened and the young children's problems are addressed at home. For some children, sadly, being in school is the better or only option but this is true if and only if these students are given a program that respects their uniqueness.

Regardless of when and why a child is enrolled, when schools provide the proper program, there is educational momentum. This creates successful and zealous students who tend to allay the fears of, and slow down, the most anxious and time-starved adults.

∼

Successful students generate their own learning.

Allen's family was very far from rich but his mother valued education, understood children and was in no hurry. When told that her son needed to spend extra time in my primary class, she was unconcerned.

When Allen finally left for third grade he had been with me for three years and it had taken all that time before he was making significant progress in reading. Along the way there had been subtle and not-so-subtle pressure from the principal and a few staff members to place Allen in special education or at least remedial reading. My take was that Allen was a normal kid who needed more time to grow up. He already was spending as much time on reading as it was prudent to do.

As time went by, the mother stopped by occasionally to update me on Allen's progress in other classrooms. After Allen entered high school his mother informed me that he had elected to study Spanish.

∼

It was my first teaching job and school started the following week. Looking for materials to teach reading, I opened the only closet in the third-grade room. Ah-ha, I thought, reading books. But it soon became clear that the only thing in the packed closet was reading books: six different sets from six different companies published in six different years. I was puzzled. All the sets were relatively modern and in good shape. Only years later did it dawn on me. When the children failed to read well, the tool was blamed. Then, a new tool was bought as a panacea, and then another and another and ...

18

The Skill, the *Only* Skill
Reading Success Through Timing

WHEN A SCHOOL OR SYSTEM respects the individuality of each child, everything reflects this attitude. A flexible structure and curriculum demand that the teaching techniques and classroom management systems also be flexible. A lack of flexibility, the most serious flaw of the assembly-line structure, is seen most easily in the teaching of reading. In no other area of education has more money, time and effort been wasted. In no other area of education have so many children been unnecessarily damaged and turned off to learning. Today, all of this is avoidable. In the past, we did not know better.

Once children began to assemble in schools, official reading instruction began in the first grade. Every child in the first grade received the same instruction, ready or not. There always were a few students who had learned to read before entrance into the grade. These students were considered superior, were not challenged but also were not stymied. Other students, considered high average or average, were ready to learn to read in the fall or, at latest, by December. Still others, the "late" and "slow" readers, posed a great and annual problem. Would they make enough progress by June to be promoted?

Although failing a young child in first grade was traumatic for students, parents (especially the father) and teacher, in the assembly-line structure there was no sure alternative. No amount of teacher effort could guarantee that a late or slow reader (both considered inferior) would catch up and satisfy the requirements of each succeeding grade. From the beginning there were many of these late and slow readers. The resulting failure created pressure to reform the teaching of reading. The first attempts involved the tools of the trade.

Long before colonial days there had been only two basic ways to teach reading. One used whole words. This highly favored method eventually would be referred to as the "look-say" method and the words learned as "sight words." Students would try to memorize a word by its combination of letters and shape. The other method, "phonics," involved the sounds of letters. From the beginning, phonics was considered the little brother to whole words. Early reform efforts, therefore, focused on materials used in the whole-word method.

Many different types of books were created to teach reading. In time, the need for different levels among books led to the creation of basal readers. Yet, the complaints of failure and underachievement continued. Workbooks were created to supplement the basal readers. They were not enough. Remedial reading lessons were introduced. This approach helped some but was ineffective with many and did not prevent the initial struggle. Those who did profit from remedial reading reached a degree of technical proficiency. However, they too often did not develop the crucial *love* of reading experienced by those who did not have to struggle.

As the years went by, more attempts were made to tinker with the basal reader. Stories that sounded more realistic than "See Dick run!" were added. Characters other than white folk were added to the stories. Poetry and other kinds of prose were added. But the stubborn reading problems remained. Teachers for years had used three reading groups per class to "manage" the students. Increasingly aware of the many differences among the children, the teachers began to break their classes down into more and more reading groups. This made it more difficult, even impossible, to read with each group every day. This violated a prime (if inaccurate) law of reading instruction.

Critics decried the use of the basal reader and blamed the

chronic reading underachievement on the basal's lack of phonics. Yet even when phonics was added, or made the primary method, groups of children still did not begin to read "on time" and make satisfactory progress.

As complaints multiplied, principals and superintendents gradually lost confidence in the teachers. This led to an increasing bureaucracy that is expensive and harmful to teacher morale and creativity. One of the first indications of this trend was the creation of a supervisory position between the principal and superintendent. Some names for this position are "curriculum coordinator" and "director of instruction." The position was not intended to be as narrowly focused as, say, the science or language coordinator of a high school. Rather, it was created to unify, coordinate and modernize the teaching and curriculums of all schools in a district. This, of course, is what the principals and superintendent are supposed to do. This added layer of supervision has not increased learning enough to justify the expense. The reading problem (among others) remains. Thus, a new teaching/supervisory position has come into vogue, the "reading (or literacy) specialist."

The creation of this position presents two problems. First, it demeans regular elementary classroom teachers and those at the secondary level who teach reading and writing every single day. Second, in many cases the key qualification for the position is having a college degree in reading or literacy. This is no guarantee of ability since these degrees demand no more rigor than other education degrees.

Of course, if the specialist (or any other supervisor) is talented in teaching and diplomacy, lesser-qualified classroom teachers can profit from the help. However, even with outstanding specialists in each and every school, they still cannot prevent significant numbers of late readers and underachievers. This is because additional supervision in reading still does not get to the heart of the problem. The true issue in reading is not "what" but "when."

The chronic controversy over reading instruction has centered on the questions "What is the best method of instruction?" and

"What materials should be used?" In fact, the two ancient methods of whole words and phonics are the only methods that work well. A good teacher, therefore, uses a combination of the two methods. Materials also should not be an issue. A good teacher uses a variety of materials to fit the students. In reality, methods and materials count a lot less than people think. This is because the key to reading is to be *developmentally mature enough* for the skill. Then, just about any tool can be used successfully, including cereal boxes and comic books.

Unfortunately, the adults continue as in the past. As more and more people are hired to micromanage the classroom teacher, private tutoring companies and makers of educational products profit from the fear of parents and educational leaders. Everyone except the teacher, it seems, has something that will solve the reading problem. Yet the problem remains as adults continue to make reading a complex and tangled issue. Perhaps someday the public will find out that learning to read can and should be easy and joyful for almost everybody.

∼

Reading success depends not on method or materials but on timing.

My family had no television until I was seven and computers and computer games had not yet been invented. Consequently, my parents and older sister read all the time and to me. When I was five and my mother noticed my ability to read a few words, she played school with me in a low-key fashion. By first grade I was ready and eager to read.

In time, my sister took me to the town library on a regular basis. She often had to vouch to the librarian that I could indeed read the upper-level books I was choosing. As my sister participated in her fifth- and sixth-grade book clubs, she allowed me to order some books from her upper-grade list. By the end of third grade I was reading far, far more at home than at school, a practice that became a habit. As an eleven-year-old I read at least one major newspaper a day and books aimed at older readers such as *Crusade in Europe* by Dwight D. Eisenhower and *The Diary of a Young Girl* by Anne Frank.

Only decades later did I realize that I (and a very few other classmates) had learned to read naturally, without the artificial pressures of time and unrealistic, arbitrary expectations.

∽

The first-grade teacher was becoming more and more tense as the students in the reading group struggled to read even the smallest and most common of words. Having a visitor (me) see the struggle was one reason, of course, for the teacher's mood but so was the calendar. It was March and it was expected that the students be showing decent progress by now. Forget the calendar, I thought. Change the material and strategy to fit the kids. The teacher pushed on doggedly, however, with her curriculum-required lesson and ended up reading virtually all the words for the frustrated students.

19

As Easy as ABC
Parental Assistance in Reading

> *"Nothing should be taught to the young unless it is not only permitted but actually demanded by their age and mental strength."*
> — John Amos Comenius
> Czech Theologian and Educator
> (1592–1670)

IT IS WELL KNOWN THAT parents play a crucial role in a child's learning. Although each child has a unique biological timetable for beginning to read, parents and other caregivers usually must stimulate intellectual growth for this timetable to be met. The things parents must do are not only easy and inexpensive but also slow down their hectic lifestyle and help unite the family.

Parents must talk to their child every day. Oral language precedes written language, and stimulation by parents is important to initiate and improve the child's talking. This can be done when doing tasks about the house, in the car or at the store. At the same time, it is just as important not to neglect speech's twin skill of listening. A common complaint in today's schools is that children have a lot to say but do not or cannot listen. In this fast and sound-polluted world, both skills obviously are more vital than ever.

A young child must be read to every day, even if only for five minutes. Older siblings or other relatives can take the place of parents occasionally. If the child shows no interest, this activity should not be forced. However, since a child imitates adult behavior, another important nudge is the parents reading regularly at home for their own purposes.

As badly as parents and teachers want a child to start reading, all adults need to show patience. A very few children begin to read on their own as early as three to four. A few more begin to read at five and even more at six. *Many* begin from six and a half to seven and a half and a few even later. Many adults go back to school and learn to read then. It is never too late to learn to read as long as the student has not been turned off to the task. But how is the parent (and teacher) supposed to know when to start formal reading instruction? That's easy. The child tells us.

The first sign is eagerness to take over the buddy reading from those who can read. At first the child may make up the words but this is a step up from listening. While "reading" or doing other tasks the child is able to concentrate for significant periods of time. As the child works, the eyes move and focus with discipline and little fatigue.

Both parents and teacher may notice that the child is learning the alphabet. It is not necessary to know all the letters to begin to read but the child must know what the letters do. Equally important, the child is able to hear and distinguish among several consonant sounds. As discussed in the next chapter, this key clue can be detected in the child's writing. Finally, the child may spontaneously pick out individual words on cereal boxes, street signs, stores, and so on. ("Hey! I know that word. It's STOP.")

Historically, the structure of schools has not allowed teachers to wait for indications of reading readiness. Consequently, alphabet, phonics and whole word instruction often are begun arbitrarily and, for many, *too soon*. Many parents naturally focus on the artificial timeline of school instruction and become very anxious for some signal of progress. This impatience is harmful and needless.

When a child begins to read naturally, educational momentum takes over. There is no stopping the child from reading everything and everywhere. When material tried is too difficult, this defeat is shrugged off. To maintain this eagerness a child should never be penalized for reading at the "wrong" time, such as when in bed with a flashlight. If a child discovers material of poor taste out of the house, correction should be low key. Parents, of course, always should model what material *is* appropriate.

As the momentum builds, different types and levels of high-quality reading material should be made available around the house and classroom. While books, newspapers and magazines are obvious choices, other types such as maps and comic books are equally valuable. All parents should take their child to the library on a regular basis. To a child who learns to love reading, a library card is gold. Having a card and reading material is of no use, however, if time is not available to read.

The only way to become a good reader is to read and read and read some more. The biggest time stealer in society is the video screen. Nothing else comes close, not even the cell phone. While a very small fraction of video viewing is highly instructive for older children (mostly from educational TV and some computer programs), *none* of it is necessary for a child's growth at *any* age. Regardless of content, each hour in front of a video screen feeds an addictive habit and is one less hour spent using the imagination, doing a hobby, interacting face to face with others, exercising and, of course, reading, reading and reading some more.

∼

Adults must stimulate but not force reading.

I spread out a month's worth of Kasha's writing left to right on the table. Her first writings only showed random letters to describe the picture she had drawn. Yesterday, however, she correctly used first consonants to represent animals in the picture. Also, the word "go" was spelled correctly.

I waited for THE question.

"When will she read?" the mother asked, as if on cue.

I pointed to the initial consonants and the correctly spelled word.

"Tasha's getting close," I answered. "She can read a few of the words that are posted around the classroom. The next stage for her writing is to add middle and ending consonants and maybe a few vowels. Then she'll probably be ready to move into books. Maybe another month or so. The writing will tell us and she'll probably ask, also."

As both parents looked over the writing they nodded. They could see Tasha's reading progress in black and white.

∼

"Could you send Jake's school work for the next two weeks home with him today?" the mother asked. "We're going on vacation tomorrow."

Not possible, I thought, since workbooks and textbooks don't drive the class and plans are adjusted daily. However ...

"I want Jake to keep a daily journal of his vacation," I countered. "When he comes back, he'll have to give a report on what he did each day."

"Great," said the mother. "I'll have him write the class some postcards, too, and bring some souvenirs home to talk about."

20

The Reading–Writing Connection
Using Writing to Monitor Reading

CRITICS ASIDE, MANY EXCELLENT and exciting changes have occurred in American education in the last few decades. One of the most dramatic has been in the teaching of writing. Much of the credit for this can be given to Dr. Donald Graves, a University of New Hampshire professor who refused to be constrained by the ivory tower.

In the late 1970s Dr. Graves and his assistants spent considerable time studying elementary students in school. They found that students write best when they are encouraged to write in a natural fashion, much as professional writers do. Specifically, a writer must brainstorm ideas, do a rough draft, rewrite to correct and polish (as often as necessary), and only then put out a final product.

This was radical thinking in an educational system that pressured students to be perfect on the first try. The thinking was right on the money and, in a rare joint epiphany, many teachers and administrators at all levels saw the worth of Graves' research. Today, the "writing process" approach is firmly entrenched in schools across the country. Although not all teachers use the approach or use it correctly, the writing process has proven itself to the point that it will not be discarded with the future ebbs and flows of education.

An unexpected asset of the writing process is its relationship to reading. For example, while it is helpful and even desirable to have various reading materials available to teach reading, in a pinch most are unnecessary. The only materials needed to teach reading are paper, pencil and crayons or markers. This is because reading can be taught using the writing process.

The advantages of using the writing process for reading are many. The process uses the tried and true techniques of phonics and whole words. However, there is an important improvement. The whole words are taken heavily from the extensive and individual spoken vocabularies of each student, especially the beginning readers. This makes the writing and reading more personal and effective. Since writing is a skill that can be done in all subject areas, the writing process can provide reading practice in a direct or indirect fashion all day long.

Primary-grade teachers love the process because it can begin long before children can read and it tells the teachers when to start formal reading instruction. To begin the writing process an individual or group art project is done (drawing is the easiest for the teacher). Then, using the art as a stimulant, each child writes at the appropriate stage of writing development. The following are just some of the stages a child goes through over time:

1. The student is prompted to dictate a story about the art project.
2. The student writes random scribbles or random letters about the art.
3. Using initial consonants, the student labels or writes a sentence about the art. (for example, B R H = The boy ran home).
4. The student uses more consonants and some vowels. Some correct spelling may appear. (The beml rn hom = The boy ran home).

It is at stage four that formal reading instruction is first effective. At that stage students' eyes are ready to differentiate among the letters and numbers and, to some extent, move from side to side and up and down. Their brains are ready to learn words and other reading skills quickly and without struggle.

As informed parents and teachers monitor the stages of the

students' writing, their ability to predict prevents a lot of destructive pressure on the parents (self generated), on the teachers (from superiors and parents) and, most importantly, on the children (from adults and from within).

Obviously, the writing process is developmentally appropriate. That is the key reason it works. It is a flexible technique that can be used to meet the individual needs of virtually all children. When the principles of the writing process and child development are blended, forced reading instruction on unready four, five and six year olds is unmasked as incompetence.

Consider the hypothetical Susie moving and entering school after the year has begun.

If Susie enters a developmental, continuous-progress school, the transition is relatively easy. The teacher tests the water to see what Susie can do in reading (and writing) by having her write a story. Regardless of Susie's age, if she shows the ability and interest to start to read or is reading already, she is given an appropriate program. If there is no readiness, Susie is stimulated with prereading activities (including the writing process) but not force fed. The teacher knows that there is no deadline for Susie to read. Susie can learn in other academic areas and in other ways while her eyes and brain mature enough for reading. Even if Susie is older and entering a higher grade, the transition is still smooth because the approach to academics is the same. First get a writing sample.

The writing process also helps prevent debates over the definition of reading and at what grade level a child is reading. Since learning to read is perceived as difficult and education's critics are everywhere, teachers and parents too often watch anxiously for any sign of reading, no matter how flimsy. Consequently, success is proclaimed when a child shows the slightest hint of beginning. This overeagerness leads to disappointment when the same child shows slow progress after the "beginning," needs remedial help and, in time, scores less than anticipated on standardized tests. It also leads to absurd statements from teachers such as, "Billy is reading well but he doesn't comprehend what he reads."

A child who truly has begun to read is obvious. The child soaks up words like a sponge and clearly understands what the words mean separately and together. When reading orally, the child is smooth and confident. The writing process shows this beginning reading when both the child and the adult can read the child's writing. The proof of beginning to read is then in black and white and without doubt.

The idea of identifying reading levels was an outgrowth of the need for teachers to gradually increase the difficulty of instruction and school's adoption of scientific-management principles. Since school was broken down into sequential work stations, the academic work also had to be labeled. Unfortunately, no one ever has agreed on how to determine reading levels.

Early on, the publishing companies exerted much indirect control of the schools. They created reading materials based on mathematical formulas involving syllables, words and sentences. The problem was that all formulas were not the same and each company was free to use any formula. Thus, a book written for a fifth grader by one company might be harder or easier than one written by another company. Also, unusual words such as those found in science, foreign languages and street slang could not be used. This made the reading material very bland and boring.

In recent years there have been attempts to redefine the levels of reading but this problem has yet to be solved. The writing process avoids this problem to a large extent. Samples of a child's writing are kept in a portfolio. Over time the portfolio increases impressively. As the eye peruses the range of the writings, the child's progress and present ability are easily sensed. This evaluation is more subjective than numerical, yet is quite valid and useful to teacher and parent. Of course, the assembly-line mentality is so strong that nothing escapes its influence, including writing.

Since the introduction of the writing process there have been ongoing efforts to bend the process to the old structure. Much time, effort and money have been spent trying to determine what students should be writing at each grade level and, lately, to tie these efforts to mandated standardized tests. Although improving the quality of writing is a necessary goal, the struggle to determine grade-level skills has taught nothing to those blinded by the old school structure.

Long ago when universal education became the norm, teaching was standardized sometimes to the point of dictating what a teacher must do in each and every situation. In theory this severe control was supposed to make it possible for supervisors to monitor their educational assembly line. It would be fair, however, to state that the teachers were not thought able to think for themselves. For example, the teachers' manuals on reading went so far as to tell teachers *exactly* what words to say to the students. School supervisors supported this micromanagement of teachers. If a reading book had one hundred pages, there were principals who expected all students to be on page fifty at midyear.

Gradually, the academic straitjacket was loosened in many school districts and experimentation and innovation were encouraged. Today, however, with the present reform movement, micromanagement has returned, especially in reading and writing. Under the guise of "literary research," some colleges are advocating that all teachers must teach reading and writing the same way. It is not that the individual teaching techniques being proposed are bad. Many are modern and quite good. It is the idea that one size fits all students and teachers that is a huge step backwards. Reading and writing clearly show the individuality of people with evidence that is impossible not to see. Yet school reform remains blind.

∽

Children's writing tells us when they will read.

Don's dog story was good news/bad news. On one hand, he finally could string more than one sentence together and make sense. On the other hand, his penmanship still needed a lot of improvement. I silently debated how to improve his penmanship without shutting him down. It had taken a lot of time and effort to get his writing this far.

I suggested to him that adding details about his dog would make the story more interesting. He agreed and for the next several minutes we worked together on descriptive words. Then I said casually, "Watch how high the stick is on the 'h.'" I demonstrated and then pointed to his paper. "Can you fix this one here and how about this one over here?" Don erased laboriously as young kids do and corrected two of the many incorrect letters.

"And by the way," I continued, "what is this chicken scratching?" I pointed again.

He giggled as he said, "It's an 'a.'"

"No way, Don! It looks like the track of a T-rex."

Don and two others listening in laughed.

Again I demonstrated the proper lower case letter.

"Try a few."

Don practiced the letter three times in the correct way. As Don went back to his other work I noted on my conference form what he had practiced.

21

Chicken Scratching
Penmanship's Developmental Component

THE ADVANTAGE TO EMPHASIZING the writing process at all levels of schooling is profound. When taught correctly, writing integrates the many language arts skills of reading, spelling, grammar, punctuation, capitalization, penmanship (if the word processor is not used for the initial draft) and public speaking. When skills are integrated, not only is teaching more efficient, the students also understand the need for learning the "smaller" skills.

The writing process also helps teachers avoid the practices of the past that made students hate writing. For example, writing used to be a favorite form of punishment. Many a misbehavior was followed by writing a punishment lesson a hundred times or more on the chalkboard or paper. Teachers who understand the writing process never use writing as a punishment, except perhaps to communicate regret to a victim of a transgression.

Using the writing process allows the teaching of penmanship without making it boring and tiring. Children are turned off to a task if it appears pointless. Filling sheet after sheet with practice letters and words is such a task and, unfortunately, still is used by many teachers. Practice does make perfect but writing-process teachers are careful to limit *isolated* penmanship practice.

Instead, they integrate the practice with another task. The smoother the practice is integrated, the better the student sees the *need* for the skill. Consider the following illustration of a teacher helping a student investigate pond water.

"Joey, I asked for a list of five bugs seen in your water sample but you've listed ten. Excellent effort. Oh, by the way, when you make a "b" be sure to close up the loop (she points). Otherwise, people can't read it. Try it a few times like this (she demonstrates at the bottom of his science paper)." He does a few letters next to hers. End of lesson.

Critics say that penmanship has suffered over the years and a few point fingers at the writing process. However, this decline was initiated by changes in society that began long before the writing process was introduced. The typewriter, telephone and word processor all reduced the use of printing and cursive writing by the average person. Present-day electronic mail, cell phones, and so on, further reduce the possibility that people will use paper and pen. Also, writing by hand of important documents is ancient history. All this makes the heavy emphasis in the past on beautiful printing and cursive writing seem antiquated and inefficient in a time-pressured world.

Schools contribute to this attitude inadvertently by emphasizing printing for only the first few years in school and replacing it quickly by cursive. Not only do many students not truly master printing, they are led to believe that cursive is superior by its emphasis. However, the only true advantage of cursive is when haste is necessary. Other than that, printing holds its own. Most of day-to-day writing (lists, record keeping, notes, and so on) can easily be done by printing and virtually all reading of documents involves print, not cursive.

The decline in penmanship has also been assisted by the mobility of the nation's people. The number of students who move during their school career is significant. Since schools differ in the method of penmanship taught, the students often do not have their original method of penmanship reenforced and sometimes must change to another method. Many students move for negative reasons and are affected emotionally. As in art, the quality of penmanship is lowered by stress in the children's lives.

In recent years the teaching of word processing in the youngest grades has contributed its share to the decline in penmanship. No one should mourn the past practice in which teachers valued beautiful strokes of the pen equally, and sometimes more, to the content of the writing. However, not only is good penmanship still necessary for communication, the discipline of achieving it carries over into other tasks. Therefore, it must not be neglected for the glitz of machines.

A favorite argument in favor of the word processor is that it makes writing more attractive to the students. This is a false argument except for the few students who have severe physical problems. When taught *correctly*, writing with pen or pencil is exciting to the students. They love using the tools of old, viewing their results and saving them for parents or other family members.

True, editing by hand can be taxing. On the other hand, the lure of overediting is a curse of the word processor. Also, adults and students alike are prone to fall into the trap of "more is better" when using machines. They forget that, as a rule, good writing is concise.

Biology give us clues for proper penmanship instruction. Although people vary as to their native ability to use tools, there is no reason why most children cannot develop decent penmanship. This includes boys. Contrary to popular belief, girls are not neater than boys. This myth arose because the average girl in any grade is a bit more mature than the average boy classmate. When penmanship (or any other skill) is introduced, the girls naturally do better because they are more ready to do the skill. Those who struggle from the beginning (mostly boys) tend to avoid using and improving the skill.

If a school respected biology, each student would be given penmanship lessons based on developmental principles. Children would practice only what they are ready to do. Those who were not ready to use pen and pencil would learn visually, orally and through manipulation.

Beginning writers would start with blank paper, especially those developmentally younger than age seven. Gesell research and unfortunate teacher experience has shown that using lines for beginners makes writing more difficult because it is unnatural for them to write on a line. Spaces should not be used since young children need the freedom of open space. Blank paper allows children to concentrate totally on the form of the letter or number. As children mature they show the ability to handle lined paper and, in fact, demand it or draw their own lines and spaces.

Once the basics were learned, penmanship lessons would be individualized and incorporated into larger lessons whenever possible. As shown earlier in the pond water investigation, it is important for students to see that neatness and precision will help *them*. Only after a child has mastered printing and cursive should the word processor be introduced. This might occur at the upper elementary level.

Other reasons support the later introduction of the word processor. Like cursive writing, the crucial advantage of the processor is speed. A person who cannot touch type (say, a young child with small and immature hands) loses much if not all of this advantage. While it is true that some people, both young and old, can get by with "hunting and pecking," this is a bad habit that should be prevented.

Economic considerations are important, also. Electronic tools are expensive to buy and maintain. Pencils and pens, although low tech, are vastly cheaper and get the job done just fine. Most important, the pace of the classroom must be controlled by the needs of the students. Machines introduced early tend to be used to justify their purchase and not because of the unique rhythm of each child.

∼

Timing, not gender, is important in penmanship.

Toby's rough draft was finished and she was preparing it for publication in the school newsletter. She spotted some words that were misused and used the thesaurus for correction. Her writing buddy, Tod, read the improved draft and nodded his approval.

The story was a fictional account of two nine-year-old best friends becoming the first girl astronauts to land on Mars. Toby's uncle had a pilot's license and likely this had inspired her choice of topic. I asked Toby to make a list of any misspelled words and enter them in her personal dictionary. They would be the core of her new spelling words. Since Toby had an interest in space, I added three "challenge" words that she didn't know: celestial, galaxy and asteroid. As soon as she felt prepared, Toby would be tested on her spelling words.

∽

The report card committee was reviewing cards from many districts. Mrs. Lasker, a well-respected fourth grade teacher from another school, waved a report card in my face. "Look at this!" she said. "This school has one grade for spelling tests and another for how the student spells while writing."

She tossed the card into the middle of the table and looked at the group. In an exasperated voice she continued. "They're on to something here. My students do well on the weekly spelling tests but they don't remember the words later when they're writing. There's no carry-over!"

22

I Before E
The Individuality of Spelling

ORAL LANGUAGE LONG PRECEDED the written word. Long before the printing press, the town crier normally was the way the average citizen learned the news of the day. His "performance" was looked upon with great anticipation. Even after the evolution of books and newspapers, the man who was a master of oratory found that this skill was one key to power. In today's world of the video screen it might seem that the long speeches of yesteryear have been replaced by visual images. Yet even within the short sound bites of TV news, the power of the spoken word is evident. Ask any politician who has come to regret a wrong phrase or even a single word. Strange as it may seem, the history of oral language in our country is connected to spelling lessons.

As American schools became established, no scientific way of teaching spelling was known. The most popular way to learn became the oral recitation method. This method was inspired by the respect adults had for those with oratory ability. Students in a class or even the whole school studied the same list of words and then orally spelled the words, one student at a time, in front of the class.

When chalk and pencil became more readily available, students wrote each spelling word several times for practice. Both of these teaching methods are still in practice today. Oral recitation remains in the form of local and national spelling bees. The writing of spelling words from lists remains exactly as it was years ago and leads up to the end-of-the-week quiz so popular with teachers.

Neither method is biologically sound, however, nor very efficient as used. Of course, a clever teacher can dress up the two methods somewhat (for example, by subtly giving the weaker bee spellers easier words) but such camouflage can only go so far.

The key to learning and refining any skill is to use it often. However, repetition alone will not ensure mastery. As noted earlier, a skill must be seen as useful in a personal way to a student. This encourages the student to work independently both in *and* out of school to learn the skill with an eagerness that "burns" the skill into the brain. When spelling is taught separately from all other skills, the need is lost on the students. Common practice today does just that.

A list of words is assigned from a commercial spelling book. The words are written several times and used in sentences. Sometimes a practice quiz precedes the real quiz given on Friday. Often a letter or number grade is assigned. The problem with this method is that many of the spelling words are forgotten quickly and the skill is not *carried over* to the writing. The futility of starting with and depending on arbitrary lists has been shown in many studies and has been known for many years. One additional proof of this futility is seen in report cards. Some school districts have two spelling grades on report cards: one for lists and another for spelling when writing!

One of the goals of the maligned "whole language" movement of years ago (not to be confused with whole words) was to integrate spelling instruction and practice with the rest of the language arts skills. Fortunately, the writing process does just that. At all grade levels a student's oral vocabulary is far greater than the student's written vocabulary. If that oral vocabulary is tapped, the writing that follows becomes personal and is far superior than that which comes from teacher-assigned topics. During the writing process the teacher notes which words are spelled incorrectly by the student. The student then works to learn the correct spellings through various short activities. The number and speed of corrections will depend on the personality of the student and the level of the class.

Several pitfalls are avoided with this personal and low-key approach. The student does not waste time on words already known. The student has incentive to learn the spellings because the missed words come from within. The student also learns intuitively that spelling is not an arbitrary adult task but is necessary for communication. Educational momentum is created immediately because each lesson is tailored individually and success is there from the start.

As children become more successful in writing and the associated spelling, it is ironic that many students then begin to demand and can profit from arbitrary spelling lists. This demand is shown by their asking for extra and "hard" spelling words and voluntarily making their own spelling lists. It is important to realize that this educational aggressiveness is caused by their track record of success. They are not afraid of temporary failure (a spelling bee to them is a fun challenge) and are not easily frustrated.

The best overall approach to spelling, however, is more straightforward. While each of us has a different potential in spelling, the more any person reads and writes, the better is the spelling. When you use the language, you learn it. Then you do not have to rely on dictionaries, spelling software in computers and faulty rules like "i before e, except after c."

~

Spelling lessons should be personal.

After Jenny dumped the glass beads onto the rug she sorted them into groups by color. I then directed her to arrange each group vertically with the longest group on her left and the shortest on her right. Now she was ready to place the groups on the graph paper.

She discovered that each graph space was large enough for one bead. "How many blue beads are there?" I asked. She touched each blue bead and correctly answered "Nine." "Color in the same number of spaces with a blue marker," I said. Jenny pushed aside the blue beads and colored in the spaces, leaving the beginning of a bar graph. "I get it," she said, and finished the graph without interruption.

∼

At the school's open house, I watched as the primary students "dragged" their parents excitedly around the room. From time to time a father would drift alone to the sand table. Each time, the father would surreptitiously look around to make sure no one was looking. Then he would dip his hands into the sand and relive his long-ago introduction to geometry.

23

Matter Over Mind
The Case for Hands-on Math

> *"The teacher and the book are no longer the only instructors; the hands, the eyes, the ears, in fact the whole body, become sources of information...."*
> — John Dewey
> American Philosopher and
> Educator (1859–1952)

IF THERE ARE UNIVERSAL languages in this world, one of them is numbers. Two people who cannot understand or speak a single word of each other's native language still can communicate mathematical ideas. Counting, for example, is one of the earliest math skills developed and it is learned early by children everywhere. This is because touching and manipulation is a natural part of any child's life and, in fact, is an impulse. At any time of day, touching and manipulation is repeated over and over if somehow a child's hands can get near physical objects, be they toys, rocks in the dirt or irreplaceable adult possessions.

Over time, children can make the transition from the concrete mathematical tasks (such as counting fence rails as they are touched) to those requiring abstract thinking and the paper and pencil that go with it. But the touching and manipulation must come first or the understanding that helps with life's more difficult math tasks may never fully develop.

Counting and other basic computational skills was the math curriculum in American schools for many years. Even at the high school level and beyond, "rapid calculation" of numbers, particularly done mentally, was a prized skill. Unfortunately, learning through touching and manipulation was not done.

Over the years, as the teaching of math changed from oral instruction to chalkboard to paper, it continued to be done in an abstract way. Children learned how to get answers to mathematical problems but it was a tedious task of memorization. Many did not understand and few cared what they were doing even when they got the right answers. In this uninspiring atmosphere, it is not surprising that students often did not develop a love for mathematics.

By the high school years many students, often female, came to believe falsely that they did not have the talent to do well in math. With the female developmental advantage, it might seem contradictory that the boys would dominate the upper-level math classes. Critics suggest that this gender domination was artificial and caused by teachers favoring attention on the more outgoing boys (that is, the boys raised their hands more often or aggressively). Experience and a little common sense indicates that most students, when introduced to math naturally and given a nurturing classroom atmosphere, can love math and do well—male and female alike.

In the last few decades the flaws of math instruction have been partially recognized. Many schools now place heavier emphasis in the lowest grades on understanding math through manipulation. At all grade levels innovative teachers have students do practical tasks of high interest and challenge that integrate math with other subject areas. For example, a teacher might teach mapping by doing a make-believe archaeological dig on school property. Or students might learn measurement skills by caring daily for classroom plants and animals. Particularly at the highest grade levels, teachers are being made more aware that their style of teaching and organization of the class must nurture all and not just those most obvious. Despite the improvements, however, all is not well in the teaching of math.

Many teachers make only a token show of being up to date. Manipulatives, for example, might be displayed all around the room in kindergarten and first grade but rarely used or abandoned early for old-style paper and pencil tasks like workbooks and "ditto sheets."

The old-style tasks can be very expensive and wasteful. Today's workbooks, for example, have slick photography, illustrations and colors to make them seem modern but tedious repetition of abstract tasks is the heart of what they have to offer. It is not unusual for principals, superintendents and even school boards to mandate the use of this inefficient tool, even in the face of objections from master teachers. To those who fear public opinion or lack imagination, the workbook represents a highly visible indication of "no nonsense" education. In the same vein, ditto sheets are still popular because they, too, appear to handle efficiently all the students while providing proof of math learning.

As students move up the grades, math textbooks eventually rule. This is not an improvement because of two reasons. First, textbooks are made by committees of outsiders. Thus, they often do not reflect local goals, values and needs. Second, textbooks are written to impress state officials in a few highly populated states. In other words, the textbooks are packaged to sell to the biggest markets. Choices for educators in all states thus are greatly reduced. Innovative teaching is not likely to be reflected in the books because it might offend the influential state officials.

This reluctance to change is based partially on how the educators themselves were educated but more so on the school structure. Especially at the secondary level, math subjects are precisely defined (for example, geometry, algebra, and so on). Each class period and the term length are set in stone. Yet, the more a lesson is hands-on, creative and challenging, the more flexible time must be. Without this approach, meeting each child's needs is impossible, even for the most dedicated and skillful teacher.

In elementary schools teachers have the flexibility to avoid the regimentation of secondary schools yet often choose to adopt the secondary structure. They break down the day into precise blocks of instructional time (9:00–9:30 Spelling, 9:30–10:15 Math, and so on) or "team teach" in some fashion with another teacher. These tactics force the elementary teachers to fight the clock just as much as in the old-fashioned high school.

Technology has been touted for years as the solution to help teachers break away from the past. However, while the calculator and computer certainly can assist in math, they are abstract tools. Early on, they work against learning. For the first several years of schooling, math is best learned when students are as physically active as possible. Machines, however, are designed to eliminate physical activity. Along with technology, the science of work also is touted as being the answer. Speed drills, for example, are supposed to be a scientific approach to managing class time by improving the useful but overused rote method of learning.

Speed drills have been used for years in classrooms, most from commercial companies and a few being home grown. Regrettably, the drills' one-size-fits-all approach and the pressure of student competition limits their benefit and is harmful to many. Yet, there *is* one available speed drill that maximizes the positive impact of rote learning by meeting the individual needs of each student. It is called Precision Teaching.

This technique, originally developed to help disabled students, matches each assignment with each student. A student competes only against himself at a challenging but not impossible level. Precision Teaching in any subject breeds success and a great desire to do more of the individualized work. When the technique is used in math, students quickly learn basic facts and operations in minimal time. Much time then is available to work on higher-level and hands-on math tasks. No expensive technology is necessary, only paper and pens for the lower elementary children and, additionally, graph paper for older students.

Of course, reform in mathematics instruction will need more than an occasional outstanding technique. Serious attempts at reform date at least from the launching of the first Russian satellite in 1957. Although these attempts do not match the track record of reading concern, the lack of progress in improving math is the same: slow, minimal and expensive. The implementation of state standards may help since higher learning skills have been mandated. However, unless the basic approach is changed and society truly welcomes new ideas, mandates alone will not create ultimate success.

The concept of moving from the concrete to the abstract must be embraced at all levels of teaching. Student goals must be based on the individual's place in a developmentally correct, sequential curriculum. Finally, all instruction must show the relationship of the math skills taught to the students' real world.

∽

Excellent math instruction requires flexible time.

The dirt from the class' worm home was divided equally among the four groups of primary students. Supervised by sixth graders, the younger students then began to search through the dirt with fingers for the wiggly creatures. Soon, piles of ten worms started to form and would be combined into hundreds and then, finally, the groups would combine their subtotals to get a final class count. If past experience held true, the total would be more than 1,000. The exercise was a good way to practice estimation. It also reinforced counting by tens for those who needed the practice while helping the advanced students to better grasp three- and four-digit numbers.

Later, after the worms and dirt had been put back into the home, each young student would be required to write about the activity and share the writing with the class.

∽

It was like a routine. Each day the science teacher of the K-8 school would take one or another of his twelve-year-old male students and walk to the office, paddle in hand. I had observed his classes several times and his discipline problems didn't surprise me. Although the school was fairly new, the science class had no equipment, no materials, no sinks and not even any windows. How could he or the principal think that corporal punishment was the solution?

24

Science Is Doing
The Relationship Between Integration and Time

FOR MANY YEARS THE SCIENCES were to be studied only at the secondary level. In some school systems this meant no earlier than seventh grade and as late as ninth. At first the students studied facts and concepts generally labeled as "science." By high school the curriculums were more specifically labeled and placed in a sequence. One typical sequence was science, biology, chemistry and physics. Often the first two courses were mandatory for all students, with chemistry and physics being for those who were expected to go to college.

In recent decades a much more varied science curriculum has been available, depending on the school system and location. Geology, botany and marine biology are examples of the additions. Also recently, science has been brought into the elementary grades. This reflects the fact that science affects everyone and, best of all, refutes an old idea that science is not for girls.

While it is noteworthy that science is now being given increased emphasis, this subject still plays a distant second fiddle to the three Rs. This can be seen in the financial and logistical support given to the subject. While many secondary schools and a few elementary schools have space designed and dedicated to science, too many schools expect the teachers to make do with general teaching space. Although the skill of a teacher is vital to any instruction, facilities with minimum space and no water, sinks, tables or storage space do not encourage superior teaching and learning of any subject, much less science.

The problem of inadequate facilities is aggravated by inadequate equipment and supplies. At all levels, teachers who teach only science have a single focus for their budget and can expect at least some support for their requests. However, elementary teachers who teach most subjects place the teaching of science far below the three Rs. This attitude and its effect on the teachers' budget is shared by many principals. The inferior status of science, especially at the elementary level, also affects how it is taught.

In the distant past, the science teacher lectured to the older students as they furiously scribbled in their notebooks. Occasionally, the teacher performed an experiment in front of the class as the students watched and continued to write. Eventually, a science textbook was supplied to supplement the lectures. Over time it was recognized by some that science instruction demands a hands-on approach. In fact, one of the allures of science always has been the use of tools. Many students today use their hands to manipulate a wide range of tools from the most basic magnifying glass to computers. Yet, a host of other students are less fortunate, as much science instruction is still grounded in the past. Some help for this inadequate situation now is available.

At first it was thought that new programs (and associated textbooks) at the high-school level were the answer. More recently, it was realized that the background and behavior of teachers of science needed to be changed for any program or tool to be effective. Thus, many secondary and elementary schools now use outside resources to upgrade their teachers and curriculum.

Science centers and their staffs, college workshops and courses designed specifically for K-12 teachers of science, and science grants from foundations are just some examples of these outside resources. In addition, there is no shortage of visual material designed for effective, modern teaching of science that can be purchased or accessed on the Internet. Yet, a whole lot more needs to be done if science instruction is to become first rate.

Again, time is crucial. At the elementary level, if teachers were to integrate their subjects they could include science each day—in theory. In reality, the near fixation on the three Rs discourages creative experimentation with integration. The historical pressure of time always has made deviation from the regular path unattractive. The recent pushdown of skills from one grade to the next lower and the addition of more non-science curriculums by well-intentioned superiors, school boards and government officials makes integration seem even riskier and less possible.

Assuming elementary teachers do have time to include science, they need an adequate background in science *before* they begin teaching. A teacher well versed in science not only is more capable of integrating science into the daily routine but is more likely to go beyond the required minimum. At the secondary level each specialty is so involved it *must* be taught by someone with that particular background. Also, secondary science teachers must be given the opportunity, through scheduling and class loads, to break away from the lecture and textbook approach and link the science subjects to the rest of the curriculum (that is, to everyday life).

It might be argued that state and federal testing in science is the official support needed to improve science instruction. However, demanding improved results does not guarantee that the system itself will be overhauled. True reform in any subject requires knowledgeable teachers. Little debated is the fact that at any level teachers with science backgrounds are difficult to recruit and just as difficult to retain. This presents a huge challenge to colleges to prepare prospective elementary teachers adequately and to school districts to compete in the general workplace for science specialists at the secondary level. One way to meet this challenge, of course, is to provide the "wiggle room" during the school day for both teachers and students to show what they can do.

Instruction is improving but reform is hindered by attitude and time.

As the third-grade class sat on the rug around me, I decided we would sing "Barges," a song I had discovered in a Girl Scout songbook. We were studying rivers in geography and the song would complement our study. The song lent itself to hand motions and the students enjoyed songs that encouraged movement.

Lily asked hopefully, "Next, can we sing 'Bingo' in Spanish?"

"Maybe later," I said. "First, I'd like to know what a barge is."

That led to a discussion of river life, tugboats, running lights and many other related topics. By the time the class finished learning the new song we had generated an impressive list of water-related vocabulary words such as starboard, fathom, hold and nautical. The discussion had gone so well it seemed prudent to teach the song "Erie Canal" the next day. I could link the song's transportation theme to "Barges" and an upcoming geography lesson on the Great Lakes. The question was how much college French could I resurrect to use in our discussion of the lakes and their relationship to Canada?

∼

Although it wasn't required, my childhood third-grade teacher taught us kids to read music and play the recorder and—wonder of wonders!—taught in a room that was originally designed for music. I can still vividly picture the special pit and blackboard for the music lessons and the huge skylight that covered almost the whole classroom. What I failed to realize was that the music room had been commandeered as a regular classroom. Years later, it would become clear that when push comes to shove, the "minor" subjects always take the hit.

25

The Three Musketeers
The Key Subjects of Art, Music and Physical Education

ART, MUSIC AND PHYSICAL education form an unlikely trio in the American educational system. They are joined together not just because of what they are but by how they are treated by the public and educational leaders. Many years ago, children of influential families received instruction in art, music and physical education (such as dancing, horseback riding and shooting) from their tutors. Their instruction was supposed to mimic the European classical education in which these three subjects were highly valued. When schools for the general public were created, however, the influence of a classical education was much diminished. It was not that the average person did not value the aesthetic aspects of life. Music, for example, was important in weekly religious worship and an integral part of the occasional social gatherings. The problem was money, time and perception.

Funds and time were too scarce to be spent on anything that was not considered necessary for daily survival. When life became easier, schools were able to add curriculums with the blessing of the community. However, the American public never has fully embraced in schools that which does not obviously lead to employment or, at least, to high status. Thus, during good economic times the subjects of art, music and physical education are supported. When times go bad, funds for these subjects are cut or eliminated.

If elementary art and music teachers have rooms to conduct

classes, they often lose these spaces due to increased school enrollment or other reasons. Exceptions are sometimes made if the rooms are specifically constructed and, thus, are undesirable for regular classes. Even this is no guarantee, however. Gymnasiums at the elementary level have been co-opted for computer labs and even partitioned into regular classrooms.

Time to hold these "special" classes also has been a chronic problem. The assembly-line structure and state laws encourage or mandate that each subject has a separate and specific amount of time for instruction. If the three Rs take up most of the day, special classes have to compete with science and other interests for the scant remaining time. Like science, it theoretically is possible to integrate art, music and physical education with the major subjects, particularly at the elementary level. However, the obstacles to integration in the present system are formidable.

Most teachers do not have the experience, talent, confidence or support to do this. At the secondary level the strict emphasis on separate subjects (and the related scheduling) makes the idea of integration almost a fantasy. Also, with state and national standardized testing being an obsession, teachers at all levels are vulnerable to the "zero defect mentality" of their superiors. In such an atmosphere, no mistakes are tolerated and, therefore, creativity and risk taking are avoided. Thus, at the secondary level the teachers' tendency to focus only on their own particular subject has become stronger, if anything.

The funds and time spent on art, music and physical education, of course, reflect the mixed perception of these subjects. Yet, all significant civilizations of the past had art, music and physical activity as part of their foundation. This great emphasis was not frivolous but was a recognition of things necessary for a vibrant existence.

This concept is understood by a small but dedicated core of American adults. Time and again, when there has been a threat to the "Three Musketeers," this core has prevented the extinction of these subjects in the schools. Some of this support has lessened the reduction of school budgets. Other efforts have found outside money and teachers until lobbying could improve or restore funding in future school budgets. Unfortunately, many adults fail to recognize that art, music and physical education have as much influence in our lives as the three Rs. The proof is all around.

It is a rare car or truck that does not have a radio, CD or cassette player. Homes are filled with expensive and extensive musical sound systems. Stores pipe music in to influence shoppers. Every film, television program and much live theatre depends on music as well as visual art. Ubiquitous advertising, a huge industry in itself, also depends on a combination of music and art to be successful. From formal architecture to home improvement, art is at the heart of the final result.

Activities such as fishing, skiing, walking and team sports are useful to promote good general health. High school, college and professional sports are prominent and enjoyed 365 days of the year. Even if people cannot recognize the intrinsic benefit of art, music and physical education in the schools, it is surprising that they do not see the link to the many and various adult jobs available in these three areas.

Some supporters of the Three Musketeers have tried to use research to prove that these subjects increase achievement in the regular subjects. Some research does point this way. One conclusion is that vigorous physical activity stimulates the body to make the brain more receptive to learning. Music and art, of course, have been shown to be excellent tools to integrate subjects and lessons and add excitement and creativity to any subject studied. However, perhaps the best proof of the worth of art, music and physical education in schools is the schools' atmosphere.

Schools that have ample programs in these subjects are more "alive" than those that skimp or eliminate the subjects. The students are happier, have better self-discipline and are better motivated to learn. Morale of the students (and staff) is higher. Vandalism is less. Many factors, of course, contribute to successful schools. But the misunderstood and slighted Three

Musketeers are as important as anything else within each and every school. If only there was time for them ...

∽

Some "minor" subjects are as vital as the three Rs.

"Watch me, Mr. Creitz!" the three six-year-old girls pleaded. I walked over to the seven-foot-high horizontal ladder. One by one the girls hung under the ladder and tried to go hand over hand from one end to the other. Abby made it easily while Gail struggled but also was successful. Liza literally was left hanging three quarters from the end and had to drop off. Back they all went to the start to go again.

∽

Several boys and girls of various ages gathered on the softball field. I watched as they chose sides and began the kickball game. There were several disputes over whether the ball was out of bounds and whether a player had been tagged with the ball. Each argument resulted in a stoppage of play but each time the game eventually resumed. After one impasse, Brian quit in disgust after not getting his way. He ran over to the swings and sat down. After pouting for a while he began to swing. Five minutes later he ran back to the field and rejoined the game.

26

Making Jack a Dull Boy
The Necessity of Play

> *"Play is the best kind of education because it practices powers of mind and body which ... would never have a chance to develop...."*
> — G. Stanley Hall
> American Psychologist and
> Educator (1844–1924)

EVERYBODY NEEDS A BREAK now and then. During the work day adults are allowed to rest and refresh themselves. Many workers even have contracts that guarantee such breaks. In this regard, elementary school children used to be treated at least as well as adults. Recess used to be a normal and significant part of each school day. This was fortunate since children have a natural urge to move and talk. Reaching, running, jumping, laughing and shouting are as natural to them as breathing. It is unrealistic and harmful to expect children to remain calm and quiet in school for long periods of time.

From the beginning, recess was recognized as a safety valve to let off physical energy pent up from sitting and bookwork. It also was a time to erase the lethargy and fatigue that was a natural result of extensive mental concentration. Both eager and reluctant students came in from recess better prepared to do more studying.

Today it is recognized by some that recess is more than just a catalyst for the classroom. Recess itself is a golden opportunity for learning to occur in a different way. The most obvious skills to be learned or improved at recess are those related to muscle strength and coordination. Better elementary schools, thus, have a large, flat, open area with grass for games and running. They also have equipment on which the children can climb and manipulate.

Ideally, these schools also would have a paved area and a wall for bouncing balls. Since children need to be alone at times and to escape from the sun and wind, trees and other places to hide also would be provided.

A good playground, thus, does not need anything complicated or expensive. A side of the school building without windows, for example, can suffice for a wall. Some equipment can be constructed by volunteers from donated and recycled materials. Equipment that must be bought does not have to be the badly overpriced "pretty" equipment now so popular with adults. Old-fashioned slides, monkey bars, and so on are much cheaper, more durable and work just as well.

The worth of recess goes beyond just physical improvement. It involves learning the three Rs apart from the regular classroom instruction. For example, at the elementary level, much math is used during play. When the students use the equipment and ball fields, estimation is practiced time and again in terms of distance, time and strength. Counting games are popular and some, such as jump roping, persist throughout the elementary grades.

Recess is also vital for social development. When children leave the confines of the classroom for free play, their world is modified or changes completely. The regular groupings of the class frequently dissolve as the students rearrange themselves according to outside interests. When recess involves other classes, the number and type of groupings is greatly expanded. With the different groups the students have unlimited opportunities to develop their social skills, including oral language. However, if a child needs "social space" and simply wants to walk about lost in thought, a good playground allows for this also and does it better than the classroom.

Among the many social skills improved during play, the most valuable is social problem solving. Mammals are programmed to play when young to practice *adult* skills and tasks, including social problem solving. Human young who do not play are in great danger of growing up to be socially handicapped adults. This alone demands that recess be an important part of each school day.

At the secondary level the assembly line's demand for frequent workstation changes works against any school-day pauses and, indeed, the opportunity for breaks of any kind are severely limited. Lunch time is notoriously short and sometimes ridiculously early. The necessity for students to move about, whether in class or not, is not a priority. Physical education never was a daily occurrence and, thus, could never make up for the rigidity of the line. At the elementary level the more primitive assembly-line structure has some flexibility to incorporate work breaks. In the last few decades, however, the elementary school has begun to resemble the high school more and more.

Public criticism of education and the resulting increased course work and pushed-down curriculums have made many principals desperate. At first this was seen at the higher elementary grades as recess was reduced to only a break at lunch. Now even the primary grades are suffering a loss as school staffs are pressured to "get those scores up." Sadly, the reaction from teachers has been silence.

The importance of recess comes into sharper focus when the home lives of the students are considered. Children do not play at home as they did in prior generations. Instead, electronics have taken the place of old-style play. Physically, mentally and socially the ill effects of this sedentary and technological life are increasing beyond the obvious and ubiquitous obesity. Some schools that value recess have organized the entire recess period to the extent of teaching their students *how* to play. Such drastic actions were necessary because many of today's students' play experience is so limited and their social skills so poor that they only drift aimlessly around the playground or are a danger to themselves or others.

The negative changes in society not only make a strong case for retaining recess at past levels, they make a case for an increase.

At the elementary level, the youngest children up to grade three need at least three twenty-minute recesses, including one at lunch. Older elementary children up to grade six need at least two, including lunch. At the secondary level, although the exact needs for the older students has not been determined (or even discussed), talk of break time might seem a waste of time. Despite scheduling woes, however, there is no reason why creativity cannot find a solution, *if* the need is recognized. Lunch, at least, should be of sufficient duration and at a decent time to allow unwinding and recharging.

It makes no sense to expect students of any age to work under conditions that have been recognized as harmful even to adult workers. Yet this is the exact situation and one that is deteriorating. If adults truly want students to perform to the best of their ability, they must not forget a painful lesson learned hundreds of years ago: "All work and no play makes Jack a dull boy."

∼

**Play stimulates crucial learning both
in and out of the classroom.**

"¿Qué día es?" asked Peggy. (What day is it?)

It was morning meeting time in the primary classroom. Peggy had volunteered to be the teacher. Several hands shot up to answer.

"Hoy es martes," said Joey. (Today is Tuesday.)

Peggy shook her head and asked, "Who can give Joey a hint?"

"Think of the moon," said Dan.

"Oh," said Joey. "I meant lunes. Hoy es lunes."

After exhausting the calendar Peggy then pointed to the students.

"¿Cuántos estudiantes hay en la clase?" (How many students are in the class?)

Some of the students looked around and started to count heads but others were long ready for the regular question.

"Veintidós (22)," said Eric confidently.

Sadie blurted out, "No, no. Samantha no está aquí. (Samantha isn't here.) Can I do the problems, Peggy?"

Sadie took a marker and wrote the following on the board:

```
   22                        11   boys
 - 1  Samantha             + 10   girls
  _____              _____
   21                        21   boys and girls
```

"Leamos, juntos," I said. (Let's read together). "Sadie, you point."

More or less together, the class read the two math problems in Spanish and for the next ten minutes continued their daily small step out of their white-bread community.

27

Speeka dee English?
Language Instruction for Everyone

FROM THE FIRST TRAVELER across the Bering Strait so many years ago, the story of America has been one of immigration. It would be difficult to find a group of the world's peoples that today is not represented in this country. With such diversity it is striking that so few native-born Americans speak more than one language. Of course, it is understandable that a single language, English, became dominant and the official language. Those who had the most power early on were from England. The domination of English became more pronounced as the second generation of all immigrant groups tended to learn English from birth (or at school entrance) and to neglect, ignore or reject the language of their parents. Third-generation immigrants became all English speaking without a look back.

For many years the loss of languages in the country was considered the natural course of history and not to be lamented. Most Americans, if they traveled at all, rarely went overseas. Thus, learning a foreign language was obviously a waste of time. The federal government reflected this feeling with the popular politics of isolationism. In time, knowing other languages was not even a priority for diplomats serving in other countries.

Some in the academic world resisted this loss of languages. In high school and college, foreign-language instruction was considered important. Latin, French, German and Spanish for decades were the main languages offered. This emphasis reflected again the roots of the country's power base. Only the high school students, however, who were considered elite were encouraged or allowed to study foreign languages. This excluded many, if not most, of the total student population.

In the 1970s as standards for students were lowered, foreign-language support waned. At more and more high schools and colleges, requirements for foreign language study were reduced or eliminated. Some of this was due to the fact that English was becoming the second language of choice internationally. Earlier British imperialism and the emergence of America as a world power after World War II had spread the use of the English language worldwide. The need for foreign language study seemed even less important than in the past. Some of this reduction also was due to the fact that learning a foreign language was considered difficult. As unmotivated, undisciplined or naive students resisted a rigorous course of study, many adults capitulated to this attitude.

On the other hand, there were some adults who went in the opposite direction. They recognized that learning a second language disciplines the mind for learning other subjects. They also recognized the danger in becoming ethnocentric and that it was important to understand and respect other cultures. Civilian jet travel and communication satellites were shrinking the world. American military and civilian personnel were active all over the globe. If Americans expected to maintain or maximize their influence in world politics and business, they would have to become more "international."

Those who supported foreign-language instruction found it difficult to find support for their position, however correct. True, over the years some secondary schools and colleges increased choices in language study to include, especially, those languages of the Far East. Any increase, however, competed with changing national politics and the swelling demand for increased emphasis on the basic subjects. Latin instruction, once a staple, continued a long decline begun years earlier. A once-great interest in French and German began to ebb. At the elementary level foreign language continued to be low priority or, more commonly, no priority at all.

There was another obstacle to foreign language instruction that remains today just as powerful as the lack of appreciation. It is the timing of initial instruction. Many years ago tutors exposed even the youngest students to foreign-language instruction. With the formation of schools, this language instruction was relegated to high school. This was almost too late. Later research indicated that, after a particular age (age six being most frequently cited), learning a foreign language becomes difficult instead of natural.

Perhaps in response to this research, language instruction eventually was offered in some systems as low as seventh grade. While some have debated the age at which the mind becomes less receptive, it can be said with certainty that the earlier a person begins language training, the easier the task will be. On the other hand, it is never to late to learn a language if perfect fluency is not the goal.

Another obstacle to language learning that may be just as important as timing is the "how" of teaching. The teaching of languages has been as much a victim of the assembly-line structure as the other subjects. Since the assembly line is strongest at the secondary level, foreign language instruction is relegated to a forty- or fifty-minute class once a day. This is a very inefficient approach.

Ideally, students should be immersed in a language all day. Acknowledgement of this is why high school and college students studying foreign languages are offered the opportunity and encouraged to study abroad. With the present structure, immersion in a language is impossible at the secondary (or collegiate) level. Some secondary schools have tried to modify their structure by reducing the number of classes per day and, thus, are able to increase the length of each remaining class. This would be an improvement if the foreign language was studied each day, but this is not necessarily the case. At the more flexible elementary level, however, immersion is less a pipe dream.

While many, if not most, teachers have studied a foreign language in high school, college or both, they usually do not feel qualified to teach the language. This is not true. As long as a teacher knows more than the students, knowledge can be passed on. Some elementary teachers independently teach what they know despite not being fluent, the subject not being part of the curriculum, the results not being measured on standardized tests and the instruction not being carried on by the teachers above. They do so because they know the invaluable nature of foreign-language learning, even if done for a short period of time.

Despite good intentions, these independent teachers are greatly influenced by the constricting nature of the assembly line. Thus, the foreign language usually is taught separately and done after the "important" subjects or as a filler. Instruction, therefore, may not be every day and often varies in duration and placement during the day. Even in the rare school that deliberately has formal instruction in some or all the grades, the approach is similar in effect. A foreign-language teacher (often fluent) comes into a classroom to conduct a whole class lesson once (rarely more times) a week. This approach is a good gesture but is only scratching the surface of what a serious program should be like.

In the developmental, continuous-progress structure, foreign-language instruction can be taught much differently. Here, the instruction is part of an integrated approach to all school subjects.

The language is taught formally or spontaneously, depending on the need. The students are required to use what has been taught as much as possible throughout the school day, both in and out of the classroom. For example, if math problems are being discussed, students must use any helpful foreign-language math vocabulary previously learned. If this is not done, the classroom teacher refuses (gently) to answer any question or grant requests. Any student who has forgotten necessary words is allowed to ask other students and then answers in the language.

Such an approach means that the students constantly are getting reenforcement for the language, gaining self-confidence as peer translators and strengthening their sense of community. It also means that the classroom teacher participates as much as the students, even if an outsider provides formal instruction. Since the language training is integrated it quickly becomes almost automatic. With the integration and flexible school structure, the teacher does not feel rushed and overwhelmed by the language inclusion.

As the year goes on it becomes obvious to the teacher that using a foreign language throughout the day does *not* steal time from the other subjects. On the contrary. When students answer in a foreign language, the students must think twice. This reenforces skills all around. The children's pride in knowing something special becomes obvious by their showing off what they know. Although a rare parent will grumble that English should be the top (that is, only) priority, many others jokingly complain that their children are speaking the language at home and teaching them.

An indication of the power of foreign-language instruction is the effect it has on students in other elementary classes who are not receiving the instruction. The "English only" students become fascinated by the foreign exchanges they hear in the hallway or when they pass by the door of a classroom with the language instruction. A good envy develops and this results in some osmosis of the language from one class to another without adult participation.

The above idea might seem a bit fanciful but even those teachers whose language instruction is a distant memory can quickly recall enough to begin the job. Teachers with no language background can learn from scratch with the children and quickly get beyond them.

It would be helpful from one point of view if all teachers in a particular school were to teach the same language. However, considering teachers' varied backgrounds, this may not be realistic. It is more likely that the students' exposure would be, for example, two consecutive years of French, three of Spanish and one each of Arabic and German in a seven-year stretch. Any combination would work out since children are flexible and the primary goals are intellectual discipline and cultural exposure—not fluency.

In a related vein, in the flexible school structure immigrant students are seen as a precious gift, rather than a burden. As the new students are immersed in English and the American way of life, they in turn share their language and customs with the class. In contrast, in today's time-pressured/English-focused schools the first thought is "Oh, no! They can't even speak English. How can we get them ready to pass the grade/standardized tests by June?"

Of course, much support would be needed by teachers for such an embrace of foreign languages. The fact that this country is experiencing its greatest immigration in many decades does not guarantee such support. In similar past situations there was great pressure for cultural assimilation and today's acrimonious battle over how to teach English to immigrants reflects this attitude. On the other hand, the politics of immigration may help to loosen rigid attitudes.

As in the past, modern politicians realize that the increasing number of immigrants means many more potential votes. In some instances political and legal leeway is being given those who have minimal or no ability to speak English. This situation (though controversial) might show society a need for more foreign-language instruction. In the long run, however, it may be one single event that will gain the needed support: the terrorist acts of September 11, 2001. Starkly revealed was a lack of language skill among our diplomatic, military and law-enforcement personnel, those who are supposed to represent and protect us. One would hope that the need to be multicultural was not lost on anyone.

∼

All students should receive daily foreign-language instruction.

Eric and Joel were finishing their final drafts of their autobiographies. I sat down next to them, opened Eric's portfolio and arranged his drafts in order. The early drafts were filled with cross outs and insertions while the final draft was almost clean.

"I noticed you using my dictionary, Eric," I said. "Did you fix those last spelling mistakes?"

Eric nodded. "I couldn't find all the words in *our* dictionaries."

"I've looked over his story," said Joel. "I think he's ready to publish it."

Eric responded, "Joel, too. He just finished his last sentence."

"Sara's mom will be in this afternoon," I said. "I want you two to sit with her while she types your stories on the computer. Ask her to print out three copies of each autobiography."

I then sent the two students to the school library. Joel had mentioned in his autobiography that he might want to be a scientist. The boys' task was to look for books on male and female scientists. Plan B was to have the librarian (if she wasn't busy) help them search the encyclopedias for similar information. We agreed that if the library did not bear adequate fruit we would go online together in the classroom. As the students departed I knew already what the boys' first search words would be if we went online: Marie Curie.

28

Nerds and Technophobes
Seduction by Tools

FOR MANY YEARS TECHNOLOGY in education was limited and primitive. Pen, pencil and ruler were it. As the twentieth century progressed and the curriculums expanded, tools were added in a limited fashion. Craft, typing and some science classes gave students the opportunity to directly use more tools as they learned. In advanced math classes, the slide rule was used. Most classes, however, never went beyond using basic writing tools.

In time, some reformers began to see emerging technology as a solution to underachievement. The film, overhead and slide projectors were introduced into classrooms but were teacher directed. Television was introduced in the 1960s and touted as a revolution in teaching. But this, too, was a passive tool. As electronic tools became more prolific and smaller in the 1970s, the tape recorder entered the classroom. With a cassette this tool easily could be used by teacher and student at all levels. However, it was not until the introduction of the computer that technology in education became obvious.

As the computer became more available in society, those who favored technology (such as computer and computer-related companies) began to advocate its use in the classroom. Historically, humans have been fascinated by technology. Thus, the advocates for the tool easily found allies in the general public for this new use. The companies' clever advertising has been heavy, ongoing and relentless for many years. The campaign has been successful by every measure and has exploited the current reform movement.

Educational leaders at all levels have jumped on the computer bandwagon. Perhaps a better term would be juggernaut because the rush to adopt the computer in schools has been hasty, wasteful and often harmful.

Every tool can be used in a constructive manner but all tools have a monetary and social price. A computer is no different. In an ideal world, careful experimentation would have taken place in the schools to see if the computer was applicable and whether the positive results (if any) were worth the price. Only then would the tool be adopted in full. The exact opposite has happened. Schools have been pressured, directly and indirectly, to embrace the computer without knowing its place in the classroom. The negative results have not been publicized or perhaps not even recognized.

Many classrooms do not have the space to properly house the equipment. The result has been overcrowding of classrooms or the "stealing" of other classrooms (such as music, art and even regular classrooms) to make computer labs. Of course, the use of laptops and wireless transmission can reduce the space problem but does not eliminate it. Computers also are very expensive. Even when donated, computers need ongoing maintenance, software and staff. While there are students without books, schools with deteriorating buildings, overcrowded classrooms, multiple portables, teacher layoffs and shortages, huge amounts of money have been diverted from tight school budgets to computer use. Few have said a word of protest or even asked for a thorough discussion on the issue.

Computer introduction also has had an unfair effect on the reputations of teachers. While some have been excited about this tool, those who have been cautious or skeptical are brushed off as old-fashioned or "technophobic." Some of this criticism is accurate. Early on, teachers developed a reputation for being helpless with audio-visual tools, even those as simple as a projector. However, at least some of the dissenting teachers have philosophical doubts. Unfortunately, these questioners are afraid to speak up or they believe it useless to do so. Indeed, who would listen to classroom teachers in the mania surrounding this hot tool? Yet an objective evaluation of the situation would reveal strong and valid reasons for the teachers' concern.

Speed, the core characteristic of computers, acts like a stimulant on computer advocates in that no speed is ever fast enough. This impatience creates an expensive obsession to upgrade equipment and software, even if the present system gets the job done. But speed in most cases is not the essence of learning. Learning has to do with contemplation, careful searching and experimentation. While learning can be a solo and isolated activity (and sometimes this is necessary), in school it usually depends on interaction among pupils, teachers and the school environment. Certainly, the computer can be used in a leisurely and interactive way. However, this is not its strength nor the reason people are drawn to the tool.

There are those who believe that computer literacy itself is a worthy goal. It is true that the computer now is used throughout world society and its use will only increase with time. However, learning to use this tool early and in school is a more modest goal than one would think. With the rise of the software industry the computer has become so easy to use that it takes little time to learn basic and intermediate skills. Consequently, there is no age cutoff by which one must start. Many computer experts see the time when all computers will operate automatically (like the one in a car's engine) or with minimal effort (for example, voice operated). Therefore, the urgency for children to learn this tool before it's "too late" is an illusion. Unfortunately, the false urgency has led to improper practices.

Teachers as low as kindergarten are being encouraged or forced to teach young children to use the computer. The belief is that with so many home computers, a child who does not become computer literate early is at a disadvantage in school and later at work. Some restate the argument by saying children need to learn at home before school entrance to keep up with or get an advantage over future school peers. Inherent in both versions is the fear of falling behind in the educational rat race. Also inherent is that the true needs of children are not understood. Consider word processing as an example.

There is no evidence that this approach creates a superior product to pencil and paper at any level. In fact, there are sound biological and sociological reasons for primary students not to use the computer *at all*, much less for word processing. Students who cannot unbutton their pants to go to the bathroom or tie their laces have more important things to do than to passively hunt and peck in front of a video screen. At least at the lower and middle elementary grades even the speed argument does not hold water. Yes, keyboard modifications might make up in part for smaller hands and younger minds but, even then, the students would not be mistaken for office secretaries.

There is a huge measure of hypocrisy and denial in the advocacy for computer use. At home and work, much discipline in the use of the tool is missing. Both children *and adults* spend a considerable percentage of computer time playing games, aimlessly surfing the net, using chat rooms and sending trivial e-mail. Even discounting the harmful content of these activities (and it is considerable), the computer is just as addictive as its cousin, the TV. Therefore, the hours spent in front of the computer by the young child are just as bad on the body, imagination and value system as the television.

A few parents severely restrict or do not allow the computer and other electronic tools in their homes. No doubt they are looked upon as quaint by others. However, when their children enter school there is no disadvantage, no penalty. Just the opposite. The children enter with the advantage of having had time to master the *vital normal tasks* of the younger child. They also enter with better manners, more patience and open minds because of less cultural and technological pollution. When a need arises for these students to use technology, they then are taught how to use it and learn quickly.

The case against early computer use is further strengthened when software is considered. At the elementary level, especially the lower grades, two kinds of software predominate. One is identical to the regular mind-numbing ditto-sheet drills and workbooks.

The other looks cute with music, color and action figures but is no more effective (or creative) than less expensive approaches of old. Some better software is available at the secondary level (for example, in music and science) and improvement at all levels is to be expected over time. It must be remembered, however, that every tool of old has been shown to have its ultimate limits and unavoidable downsides. No new software program will eliminate those of the computer.

Despite the pitfalls of the computer and its bandwagon, only a shortsighted person would underestimate the potential worth of any tool. If technology can allow handicapped students to participate in the regular classroom, it certainly can assist regular students. Consider, for example, the resources available for research on the Internet and the ability of students to instantly communicate with others around the world. On the other hand, there is no proof that the computer is superior (or even equal?) to the best teaching methods involving low technology or none at all.

The introduction of the computer has hidden the fact that less glitzy technology had previously made many changes in the classroom, both good and bad. Central heating, electricity, indoor plumbing, pencils and sharpeners, ball point pens, calculators ... the list is quite long of the technology that has had an impact on learning. Whether each type of technology has been good or bad for learning has depended on it being in sync with the natural rhythm of learning. Two hundred years of experience has shown that the best learning occurs when teachers and students take *time* to interact face to face, regardless of physical facilities and equipment. That is why, when adults reflect back on their school days, their memories are first of their friends and teachers, not the tools.

Technology is most useful when it is in sync with the natural rhythm of learning.

Otis had been very disruptive and aggressive in kindergarten. Observers couldn't help but think (with guilt) that Otis would land behind bars down the road.

By the time Otis arrived in my primary class he had been coded as having emotional problems. It was tempting to let the special education teachers keep Otis out of the room for most of the day. His biggest need, however, was to learn how to coexist in a group. The hitch, of course, was how to protect the education of all the others. The solution was in the class structure.

Flexible time allowed Otis to study at a rate best for him. He was given assignments within his ability, many of which were high interest and involving physical movement. Unless the entire class was listening to me or another student, Otis (like the others) was allowed to move about the room quietly without permission. If he was really uptight, he could go into the tiny teaching cubicle adjoining the classroom and "escape" for a few minutes. Or he could do an activity like the water table or easel and physically work out his frustrations.

If Otis' behavior was significantly improper he was taken by my aide or a volunteer out of the room for a short time. As Otis' three years with me progressed, however, this last tactic was used less and less. He learned that there was far too much he liked to do in the classroom to risk banishment.

29

An Ounce of Prevention
The Abuse of Remedial Services

IN THEORY AND IN GENERAL practice, the 1975 federal law that mandated proper educational help for the disabled was beneficial. However, it had an unintentional side effect. As touched on earlier, the mandate was so complex and time consuming that it hindered the operation of schools. More than a few well-qualified special-education teachers quit their specialty to go back to the regular classroom largely because of frustration with the process. Another factor was that they knew many of their charges basically were normal students who, if handled better in the regular classroom, would not have to be labeled.

To the relief of educators, the federal law was eventually revised to streamline the entire special education process and make it more practical for schools to follow. The revision also addressed the unnecessary coding of students. However, the process still is formidable, and with No Child Left Behind to the forefront and the present structure of schools, it would be naive to think all incorrect coding will be eliminated. Sad to say, politics alone makes such coding attractive. There is less fallout if students who produce lower scores on standardized tests have special-education labels.

So, how can conscientious schools and parents avoid the pitfalls of the No Child Left Behind/special-education law combo? Asking the following questions about each struggling student is a good start:

1. Is a student with difficulty in the proper grade? In developmentally based schools the question would be, "Is the student receiving the correct program of study?"
2. Is the student with the proper teacher? Sometimes a teaching style does not mix with a student's learning style or personality.
3. Does the student have undetected vision, hearing or other kinds of physical problems? Although schools screen early for these problems, more investigation may be needed.
4. Does the student have the intelligence to learn the skill or subject? Intelligence (and talent) take many forms. It is not a sign of weakness to find a skill or subject difficult.
5. Does the student want to learn what is being taught? A student's interests can be encouraged but not forced, even in subjects adults consider most important.

When it has been determined that a student needs and could benefit from extra help, it is best if the student receives the help *within* the classroom and by an adult or other students from that room. The goal is to not make a student feel isolated or singled out in a negative way. If the person delivering the services is an outsider, the first choice of location still should be within the regular classroom. This is true even if the child is identified as having a disability and legally must be serviced by a special-education teacher.

Sometimes, however, the classroom is too small or the student is too easily distracted. Then it is proper for the student to leave the class for instruction. Care must be taken, however, not to have the child leave the regular classroom too often or for too long. When absent, a child risks losing the feeling of class identity, which is important for social and emotional stability and growth.

As the necessary extra help is provided, it must be used as

if it were scarce and irreplaceable, only at the right time and in the right amount. One reason for this caution is logistical. Funds, space and adults ultimately are limited. More important, though, children can have their short- and long-term progress slowed if they become dependent on others.

Unfortunately, a few students do have actual learning disabilities. The disabilities can be very difficult and, sometimes, impossible to overcome. Of course, no one should ever take a defeatist attitude towards any child's learning. On the other hand, parents and lawmakers sometimes expect too much. A lot of useless student struggle and adult acrimony can be avoided if the educational program focuses heaviest on what the child can do and lightest on what is less possible. Consider the most emphasized skill as a prime example.

Because of the overreliance on reading by curriculums and teachers, not being able to read in today's schools usually is educationally fatal. Thus, no one would argue against the importance of reading. Yet there *are* other ways to learn. The best educational program, therefore, is flexible in its approach.

As time goes by, if there is reasonable hope a child in question will learn to read, regular and remedial efforts should be made. However, the efforts should never use the same old tired and worn out approaches that did not work in the first place. Also, the reading instruction should be a lesser portion of the school day. Most effort should be made to have the child learn the other subjects by ear, manipulatively and visually (such as using graphs, photos, charts, and so on) as part of the regular classroom.

This change in emphasis and technique for those not reading or struggling to improve would be regarded as nothing short of heresy by many outsiders and teachers, alike. ("How dare the school give up on Joey's reading!") Feathers also would be ruffled because the need for teachers to break away from their dependency on texts, the copier and every student doing the same thing at the same time would be crystal clear. This, in turn, would have far reaching implications. Report cards would have to change to reflect the emphasis on success, rather than failure. Adults would stop wasting time and money on the improbable or impossible. But it could be done. The reward would come with everyone, especially the students, recognizing how much each student can learn, even ones with significant difficulties.

∼

Remediation should not dominate a child's school day.

The new school-board policy was an official acknowledgement that the grade-level expectations did not match the development of many students. Those expecting to enter kindergarten in September now had to be five by the *previous* April 1, the earliest in America's schools. Children with their fifth birthdays from April 2 to August 31 would be considered for enrollment if they were evaluated developmentally as being at kindergarten level. Exceptions would be made for children with significant problems or difficult home situations. It was understood that some, perhaps all, of these exceptions would need extra time before first grade.

∽

Two news items surfaced at the same time. The first item was about the abysmal teaching salaries in Maine. The governor was championing a beginning salary of at least $30,000 in every school district. He didn't mention, of course, that those in many other professions already start much, much higher. The second item was about the NBA. Or was it the NFL or MLB? No matter. The report was that the average salary for all the league's players was now $3,000,000. Now, I've never met a teacher who said she went into it for the money but I know some who left because they couldn't pay the bills. Worse, I know a bunch who quit because they weren't allowed to use the brains that they were born with.

30

Fertile Soil
Nurturing and Protecting Innovation

> *"To detect the moment of the instinctive readiness for the subject is, then, the first duty of every educator."*
>
> — William James
> American Psychologist and
> Teacher (1842–1910)

WITH THE CONSTANT CRITICISM of American education, especially in the last decade or so, it is easy to overlook the progress since colonial days. Children no longer are humiliated by sitting in a corner with a dunce cap. Some schools still try to motivate by striking the students but the practice is dying out. In past years students with significant problems were denied education or swept under the rug. Today they are recognized, at least officially, as equal members of the school community.

Years ago at all levels, teachers rigidly directed every step of learning. Today, some of the teaching methods used and assignments that modern students receive would be looked upon with envy by yesterday's students and teachers. This positive change has not been by accident. Throughout the history of American education there always have been those who tried to improve the situation.

The question remains, however, as to why progress has been so slow, limited and fragile. The problem is a lack of fertile soil. Regardless of good intentions and talent, no farmer can succeed in the long run without this most basic need. So, too, American education will not truly succeed until the structure encourages and protects innovation.

Some not in education might advocate that the present reform movement provides fertile soil. Aren't achievement levels in public schools improving, dropouts declining, and so on? Well, not exactly. There has been some improvement in some schools in some categories but no dramatic improvement anywhere, much less across the board.

If the soil was fertile, it would be *obvious* to everyone. Parents would be clamoring to keep or put their children into the public school systems. Yet, the opposite is true. An increasing number are trying charter schools, private schools or home schooling despite evidence that the alternatives (particularly the charter and private schools) do not have the answers either.

If the soil was fertile, recruitment *and* retention of highly qualified leaders and teachers would be easy. Yet, the opposite is true, even in many private schools. To reverse this situation, obviously the profession must be made more attractive. Improving the quality of teachers has been proposed as part of the answer. The seriously flawed "master teacher" certification is one new approach encouraged at the local level. State governments use various approaches including the old (and minimally useful) demand that teachers go back to college periodically. Testing, testing and more college courses is the uninspired direction in which the federal government is going.

If any effective method of educator improvement or recruitment does come along, it paradoxically may work against the retention of *outstanding* educators. How many master craftsmen will work long in a substandard facility with minimal supplies, equipment and budget? How many outstanding craftsmen will work long for minimal pay and no prestige? And most important of all, how many outstanding craftsmen will work long in a situation where they do not have a strong voice in policy and the freedom to use their wide range of talents?

To attract and retain good teachers and leaders, working in

schools must be seen as special. As long as students and educators are slaves to artificial restraints such as the clock and paying lip service to the individuality of kids, this will not happen. The visitor to the farm and artisan workshop tends to romanticize the life of the craftsman. Yet, one impression is accurate: the master craftsman works to a natural rhythm that breeds success. Likewise, paying attention to the individual rhythm of each child breeds similar success in the classroom. This success proves that with the fertile soil of the proper school structure, learning is limited only by the imagination and courage of the adults and children.

∽

**A nurturing environment is crucial for
both student and educator.**

The private kindergarten teacher dropped by my room after school for a chat. Over the years she had recommended to her students' parents that they choose my (public) primary class.

"You'll be getting Justine next year," she said. "She needs a lot of TLC. Her dad died when she was young. Recently, her mother skipped town, leaving Justine with the grandparents."

Later, when the teacher brought Justine to school for a visit, I evaluated the six-year-old. She was physically six but academically and, not surprisingly, emotionally she wasn't close. When I put out the annual call for volunteers, Justine's grandfather responded. A product of the "old school," he was deeply worried at first by Justine's initial progress and the developmental approach. However, by the end of the year the grandfather was able to see the rationale of the class structure and how all the students were eager and successful. After a second year in my first-grade room, Justine went on to second grade. The grandfather, however, stayed behind to volunteer for a third year in my room.

∽

The primary-grade teachers had just about completed an open discussion with a group of parents about child development. We had emphasized that if you want to ensure school success, you give a child enough time to learn. It is better to graduate later successfully than to struggle through at the regular age or—worse!—to fail. One father had not made one comment all night but his body language said it all. He didn't buy a word of it. Finally, he spoke. "If my child doesn't graduate on time at eighteen, that means he will earn one year's salary less during his lifetime!"

31

All the Time in the World
Time and Timing as the Most Crucial Resource

THERE HAS NEVER BEEN A shortage of snake oil salesmen. Their primary targets have always been the most desperate: those with physical or emotional pain. Today, they pitch educational products and services at anxious parents and school officials. Their words are just as alluring and filled with half truths and deceptions as those who worked out of horse and wagon many years ago. In the past when suspicious adults examined their snake oil, they discovered that its ingredients at best were nothing out of the ordinary. At worst, the ingredients were like poison.

Educational snake oil, too, offers old or harmful ingredients and promises miracles that it *never* has been able to deliver. This pattern of failure does not deter the salesmen or the buyers. The salesmen simply repackage the old oil and work up a new pitch. Citizens unaware of or ignoring past deceptions continue to look for that one cure for American education. There is no quick and easy commercial fix for what ails the American educational system. No new phonics game or educational "institute" hawked over radio and TV can cure it. Likewise, trying to remake education into a business is a futile gesture.

Snake oil of the past often contained opium that seemed to help by distorting reality and dulling the pain. Once the drug wore off, however, the original problem remained. In education, the opiates of more money and effort remain key ingredients of educational snake oil. They, too, distort reality. They, too, bring some temporary change to a bad situation but wear off in the long run.

And they, too, do not get to the underlying problems, even when stirred with the most modern and glitzy of electronic tools.

The history of American education is a study in ironies. One of the greatest is the call for higher educational standards and accountability even as the personal conduct and discipline of many adults in society is declining. While schools are supposed to model and teach the ideal, they still reflect society at large where children imitate the adults.

A second irony is the use of standardized tests as the main and often sole way to judge students, educators and schools. This attempt at accountability is itself "uncreative" and discourages innovative teaching and learning beyond what might be on THE test.

Another irony is that signs demanding dramatic and creative change to education are many, everywhere and obvious ... but we do not see. The mobility of the people is one such sign. It does not shock teachers anymore for a child to leave class in October for a school in another town, come back in February and leave again in May. Even in a stable family, children who start kindergarten in Brooklyn may graduate from high school in Nebraska with a stop in Florida along the way. This is due to a trend in adults to have more than one occupation (sometimes several) during a lifetime. Therefore, schools must adopt a generic flexibility that can handle and prepare students for such mobility.

A fourth irony is that as outsiders pile on classroom expectations, more is truly less. A visit to a typical elementary room, for example, would reveal a thick binder for each curriculum taught by the teacher. The sum of the curriculums is so overwhelming that not even Superteacher could get through the required work in a school year, even *if* all the students were ready to learn the skills.

The obese curriculums reflect, in part, the idea that schooling is a race against time to learn all knowledge (or that which is crucial) before high school graduation. Yet, contrary to popular belief, adults do not know exactly what skills by graduation are necessary for success in the future world. There is agreement on some skills in a general sense ("Children must learn to read") but no precise list or endpoint for each skill can be agreed upon or supported by proof. The reality of school years, diplomas and degrees is that at best they are only general benchmarks of accomplishment. Even when attained, each of these benchmarks is only a stepping stone in a necessary lifetime of learning. Therefore, students and teachers would profit much more if fewer skills were taught but taught better.

Teachers would have the *time* to meet the needs of the individual students instead of rushing on to the next skill required by the curriculum. Students would have the *time* to overcome obstacles and to investigate a particular skill in depth. Both students and teachers would have the *time* to go off on the spontaneous tangents (sparked by their individual experiences and interests) that stimulate tremendous learning and are remembered by students until their dying days. Educational momentum eventually would sweep most students well beyond the minimum requirements. The positive attitude generated would by itself justify the slimming down of curriculums since motivated children do most of their learning out of school.

The idea that learning must be ongoing for life no longer is debated. What must be recognized next is that, in the destructive rat race of modern childhood, more time must be found within the regular school day and year for children to learn as individuals. A cynic would say this is the cruelest of educational ironies: we resist giving children time to learn in school but are all too willing to give them time as adults, say "twenty to life," when their lack of education hits home. And the cynic would have a point. What is the rush, anyway, in the childhood years? With a little luck each child will reach more than three score and ten years, all the time in the world.

The resource of time and timing is the key to true reform.

Index

abuse: effects on students, 54, 59–60, 71; substance, 38
addiction to computers and television, 160
alcohol, 40, 81, 102
Ames, Dr. Louise Bates, 24
art as screening tool, 82
arts, importance of, 139, 140–143
assembly-line model of education 21, 37, 64–65, 68; definition of, 17; greatest flaw in, 106; and foreign-language instruction, 152

basal readers, 107–108
behavior problems: increasing, 73, 80–83; violent, 74, 81
bell curve theory: definition, 42; 53, 85, 96
biology, effects on learning, 53–57; 59–60
Boulder study, to measure developmental approach, 30
brain development, 54–55
business, decline of: effects on educational reform, 35, 77

charter schools, 169
child development. *See* development, child
child labor, 17
coding, 67, 163
college enrollment, declining standards, 78
competitiveness, problems of, 73
computers: addiction to, 160; hazards of, 73, 102–103, 158–161; software, 160–161; use in education, 156, 157–161

core courses: expanding of, 94, 95–96; weakening of, 78
creativity, lack of in educators, 38–39
curriculums: expanding, 94–95, 173–174; and modern dangers, 102; need for individualized, 95–99; standardized, 37

denial of problems in education, 85–88
dental development. *See* teeth
development, child: early theorists and reformers, 20–22; emotional, 55–56; four aspects of, 54–57; intellectual, 54–55; physical, 54, 58, 59–62; social, 55–56; universal pattern of, 59
developmental approach, 23, 24–27; abandoning, 28; early successes, 35–36; early theorists and reformers, 20–22; educators' lack of skill, 31; and foreign-language instruction, 153–155; research, 30–33; in teaching penmanship, 123–124
developmental strain, 59–62
developmental testing, 25, 56, 98; racial and class bias in, 30–31; using art in, 82
Dewey, John, 20, 21
disabilities, learning, 32, 59, 163–166
disabled students, services for, 163–166
drugs, 73, 76, 81, 102

education, history of. *See* history of education
effort, increased, 36–48
electronic tools: hazards of, 73, 102–103; and penmanship, 124; use in education, 156, 157–161

elite students, 15; decline of, 44, 77–83, 151
emotional development, 55–56
emotional problems, 80–83
enrollment: developmental, 167; later, 104
evaluation: of schools, 91–93; of special needs students, 163–164
extra time, 14, 23, 25–27, 30–33, 36, 52, 58, 65, 84, 99, 104, 105, 167, 171; and flawed research, 32; negative (Boulder) study, 30; and premature birth, 58
eyes and forced learning, 61–62

failing a grade. See extra time
family problems, effects on students of, 79
fatigue: among high school students, 79; and recess, 145
flexibility, 97–99; discouraged in schools, 64–65; and learning disabilities, 165–166; in learning to read, 106; need for, 70, 71–75; and student mobility, 173
forced learning, dangers of, 58, 59–62
foreign-language instruction, 78, 149, 150–155; methods, 152–155
freedom of choice, problem with, 75
funding: and the arts, 140–143; cuts of the 1990s, 38; how to manage, 37; state rulings on, 84

gender and penmanship, 123
Gesell Institute of Human Development, 22, 24–26, 29, 31; and eyesight research, 61; using art as screening tool, 82
Gesell, Arnold, 20–22, 24–26
GI Bill as example of extra time, 26
gifted and talented programs, 76, 78
glasses, forced learning and early use of, 61
grade inflation, 78

grade placement: child development and, 52–57; chronological, 53, 96; primary teacher's role in, 25; by reading readiness, 58. See also overplacement; extra time
Graves, Dr. Donald, 115
guidance counselors, increasing numbers, 75
guns in schools, 81

handicapped students: integration of, 66–67; labeled as, 60
hands-on instruction: math, 129, 130–134; science, 135
Head Start, 71–72, 102
held back a grade. See extra time
history of education: early U.S. school system, 15–18; funding, 37; ironies in, 173; poor leadership in, 41–45; study of in teacher preparation, 87
home schooling, 75, 169
homework, excessive, 37, 79
homicidal violence, increasing, 74
hothousing, negative effects of, 60–62
hyperactivity, 80

immersion, foreign-language, 152
immigrants: and foreign-language instruction, 154–155; and language diversity, 150; placement of, 97; recent wave of, 68
industrial model of education. See assembly-line model
Industrial Revolution, effects on education, 17–18
industry, decline of: effects on educational reform. See business, decline of
innovation in education, 167, 168–170
intellectual development, 54–55

kindergarten, purpose of, 101
knives in schools, 81

labor, child, 17
language instruction, foreign, 149, 150–155
late bloomers, 56
later enrollment, 104. See also extra time
leadership in education, 40–45; history of, 41–44; selection of leaders, 42–44
learning disabilities, 11, 32, 163–166; and premature birth, 59
learning, forced, 59–62
learning, lifetime, 11
least restrictive option, 66
lifelong learning, 11, 174
literacy specialist, 108
locomotion, universal pattern of, 59
look-say method, 107
lunch time, 147

mandates, state and federal, 38, 45, 63, 67, 71, 79,
Mann, Horace, 16
master teacher certification, 169
materialism, problems of, 72, 73
math instruction, 129, 130–134
maturation, forced, 59–62
medical model, 65–69, 96
minimum competencies, 77–78
mobility, increasing student, 70, 173; effects on penmanship, 122
momentum, educational: in learning to read, 112–113; negative, 64–69; positive, 101–104, 174; in spelling, 128
music instruction, 95, 139, 140–143

No Child Left Behind, 78, 163

Okies, new, 70
open classrooms, 29–30, 36
openness of schools, 92–93
outreach programs, 91
overplacement, 14, 25–27

panaceas. See computers; effort; spending
parents: and access to school, 92, 93; and anxiety, 101–102; assisting with reading instruction, 110, 111–13; decreasing influence of, 74–75; effects of immature, 72; expecting too much, 56, 62, 165; and Head Start, 71; lifestyle of, 76; need for simplified lives, 79; and outreach programs, 91; positive influence of, 102–103; and computer access, 73, 160
penmanship: and gender, 123; developmental instruction, 120, 121–124; readiness, 19, 52
phonics, 107, 108, 109, 112; in writing process approach, 116
physical activity, importance of, 145–146
physical development, child's, 54
physical education, 37; importance of, 140–143
Piaget, Jean, 20–22
play time: lack of, 37; necessity of, 144, 145–148
poverty, 31, 36, 55, 59–60, 65, 80, 81
Precision Teaching, 133
premature birth: effects on development, 59; and grade placement, 58; straining school system, 72
private schools, 75, 169
psychological problems, increasing, 80–83

racial and class bias, 30–31
raising the bar, 36–39, 69, 95
readers, late and slow, 106–107
readiness, reading. See reading readiness
reading instruction: history of, 106–109; using writing process approach, 115–119

177

reading readiness, 10, 19, 94; and brain development, 54–55; early signs of, 112; and incorrect grade placement, 58; and learning disabilities, 163–166; and physical development, 54; and remedial services, 63; and rigidity of school system, 14; written signs of, 114; and writing, 115–119

reading specialist, 108

recess, 34, 37, 62, 100, 103, 145–148

reform, educational: current movement, 77–79, 85–88; developmental reform movement, 24–27, 29–33; failures of, 11–13, 35–39; first step toward, 13, 87; movement during the 1800s, 16–18; public involvement in, 85–88

remedial penmanship, 19

remedial reading, 17–18, 63, 65; introduction of, 107

remedial services, 59–60, 63, 162, 163–166; and medical model, 65–69

report cards, 36, 57, 60, 65, 66, 165; and spelling, 127

research on developmental approach, 30–33

research, educational: history of, 20–22

science instruction, 43, 95, 135, 136–138

scientific management approach, 17, 63, 64–69, 96–97. *See also* assembly-line model of education; medical model

sedentary lifestyle, 80, 147

sexual behavior, improper, 81

shootings, 74, 81

sight words, 107

skills, universal pattern of development, 59

slowing down, need for, 79, 102–103, 104, 111

social development, 55–56; during play time, 146–148; Gesell and, 21

social problems, 80–83

software, computer, 158, 159, 160–161

special education, 36, 66–67, 105, 162, 163–166

speed drills, math, 133

speed: computers and, 124, 159; harmful effects of, 73

spelling, 121, 125, 126–128, 156; and writing process approach, 127–128; *Webster's Blueback Speller*, 16

spending, increased, 35, 37–38

standards, state and federal mandated, 79, 134

state rulings on education, 84

strain, developmental, 59–62

stress, 31; assembly line and, 17; emotional effects of, 55; forced maturation and, 61–62; past and present, 80; physical development and, 54; poverty and, 31, 81; penmanship and, 122; and separated parents, 79

student teaching, 48–49, 50

substance abuse, 38

suicide, 81

teacher preparation programs: history of, 21, 47–49; new methods in, 168–170; recent reforms of, 49–51; and student teaching, 48–49

teachers: breakdown among, 68; evaluation of, 42; recruiting and retaining, 169–170; role during 1800s, 16; salaries, 167; in science, 13; strengths and weaknesses, 46–51; walk-by evaluations of, 92–93

technology: hazards of, 72, 73, 102–103; and materialism, 73; in math instruction, 133; use in education, 156, 157–161

teeth as developmental markers, 10, 84

test scores, 34, 37, 44, 93

testing, developmental, 23, 25–26, 52; and racial and class bias, 30

testing, standardized, 30, 32, 37, 44, 65, 79, 117, 119, 141, 153, 163, 173
testing, state and federal mandated, 38, 78, 79–80, 138
theories of education, early, 20

violence: effects on students, 55, 68; increase in schools, 74–75, 81; observed by Horace Mann, 16
vision and forced learning, 61–62
vocabulary instruction, 127, 139
volunteers in schools, 92, 146, 171

walk-by evaluations, 92–93
weapons in schools, 81
Webster's Blueback Speller, 16
whole words method, 107, 109; in writing process approach, 116
word processing, 159–160; effects on penmanship, 122–123, 124
workbooks: inappropriate use of, 34, 114; for math instruction, 132; for reading instruction, 107
workplace, decline of, effects on educational reform. *See* business, decline of
writing process approach, 115–119

Author's Notes

Precision Teaching was created by Dr. Ogden Lindsley, et al. in 1965. Further information can be obtained from the Standard Celeration Society at www.celeration.org.

Dr. Donald Graves has published many books on the Writing Process. They are available at local schools, bookstores and on the Internet.

Many books on child development by the original staff of the Gesell Institute are available at bookstores and on the Internet. The Gesell Institute has a website with information on services or can be called at 203–777–3481.